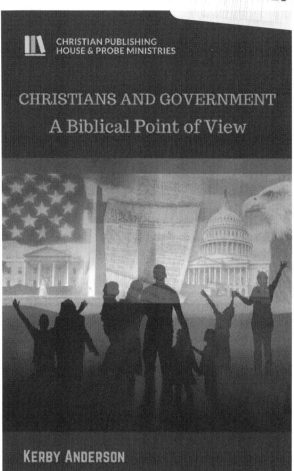

CHRISTIAN PUBLISHING
HOUSE & PROBE MINISTRIES

CHRISTIANS AND GOVERNMENT
A Biblical Point of View

KERBY ANDERSON

CHRISTIANS AND GOVERNMENT

A Biblical Point of View

Kerby Anderson

Christian Publishing House

Cambridge, Ohio

Christian Publishing House

Professional Conservative Christian
Publishing of the Good News!

CPH Since 2005

Unless otherwise stated, Scripture quotations are from *New American Standard Bible (NASB)* Copyright © 1960, 1962, 1963, 1968, 1971, 1972, 1973, 1975, 1977, **1995** by The Lockman Foundation

CHRISTIANS AND GOVERNMENT A Biblical Point of View by Kerby Anderson

ISBN-13: 978-1-945757-00-6

ISBN-10: 1-945757-00-0

Table of Contents

Kerby Anderson

Kerby Anderson is the President of Probe Ministries. He holds masters degrees from Yale University (science) and Georgetown University (government).

He also serves as a visiting professor at Dallas Theological Seminary and has spoken on dozens of university campuses including University of Michigan, Vanderbilt University, Princeton University, Johns Hopkins University, University of Colorado and University of Texas.

He is the author of thirteen books including *Signs of Warning, Signs of Hope, Moral Dilemmas, Christian Ethics in Plain Language, A Biblical Point of View on Islam, A Biblical Point of View on Homosexuality, A Biblical Point of View on Intelligent Design, A Biblical Point of View on Spiritual Warfare*, and *Managing Your Money in Tough Times*. He is also the editor of many books including *Marriage, Family, & Sexuality* and *Technology, Spirituality, & Social Trends*.

He is the host of "Point of View" radio talk show and regular guest on "Fire Away" (American Family Radio). He has appeared or numerous radio and TV talk shows including the "MacNeil/Lehrer News Hour," "Focus on the Family," "Beverly LaHaye Live," and "The 700 Club."

He produces a daily syndicated radio commentary and writes editorials that have appeared in the *Dallas Morning News*, the *Miami Herald*, the *San Jose Mercury*, and the *Houston Post*. His radio commentaries have been syndicated by International Media Services, United Press International, American Family Radio, Moody Radio, and the USA Radio Network.

Kerby is married to Susanne and is the father of three grown children.

Preface

How should Christians think about government? Laws and government policies affect our daily lives, yet most of us do not think too much about how to apply biblical principles to politics and government.

The Bible teaches us that government is a divinely ordained institution (Romans 13:1–7) and that it is ultimately under God's control. It is the only institution that is given the power of the sword: the sword of justice (to punish criminals), the sword of order (to thwart rebellion), and the sword of war (to defend the country).

The following chapters originally aired as Probe Ministries radio programs and have been edited into chapters that address various aspects of government. The first section sets forth the biblical principles about government and then applies these principles to the American government. The second section sets forth the founding principles of the American experience. This includes an examination of the Declaration of Independence, the Constitution, the Bill of Rights, and the Federalist Papers.

The third section deals with church and state issues. The fourth section looks are various aspects of political debate and discourse. The final section provides a brief overview of the Christian heritage of this nation that was important in the founding of this country and the framing of our founding documents.

As Christians, we need a clear understanding of our roles and responsibilities within the government. We need to understand our origins and apply biblical principles to our social and political engagement. It is my hope that this book will inform you and challenge you to be a better citizen and become the salt and light (Matthew 5:13-16) that Jesus called all of us to be in the world.

2

SECTION 1 Christian Principles

CHAPTER 1 Christian View of Government and Law

Christian View of Government

Government affects our lives daily. It tells us how fast to drive. It regulates our commerce. It protects us from foreign and domestic strife. Yet we rarely take the time to consider its basic function. What is a biblical view of government? Why do we have a government? What kind of government does the Bible allow?

Developing a Christian view of government is difficult since the Bible does not provide an exhaustive treatment of government. This itself is perhaps instructive and provides some latitude for these institutions to reflect the needs and demands of particular cultural situations. Because the Bible does not speak directly to every area of political discussion, Christians often hold different views on particular political issues. However, Christians are not free to believe whatever they want. Christians should not abandon the Bible when they begin to think about these issues because there is a great deal of biblical material that can be used to judge particular political options.

The Old Testament teaches that God established government after the flood (Gen. 9:6). And the Old Testament provides clear guidelines for the development of a theocracy in which God was the head of government. These guidelines, however, were written for particular circumstances involving a covenant people chosen by God. These guidelines do not apply today because our modern governments are not the direct inheritors of the promises God made to the nation of Israel.

Apart from that unique situation, the Bible does not propose nor endorse any specific political system. The

Bible, however, does provide a basis for evaluating various political philosophies because it clearly delineates a view of human nature. And every political theory rests on a particular view of human nature.

Human Nature

The Bible describes two elements of human nature. This viewpoint is helpful in judging government systems. Because humans are created in the image of God (Gen. 1:26–27), they are able to exercise judgment and rationality. However, humans are also fallen creatures (Gen. 3). This human sinfulness (Rom. 3:23) has therefore created a need to control evil and sinful human behavior through civil government.

Many theologians have suggested that the only reason we have government today is to control sinful behavior because of the Fall. But there is every indication that government would have existed even if we lived in a sinless world. For example, there seems to be some structuring of authority in the Garden (Gen. 1–2). The Bible also speaks of the angelic host as being organized into levels of authority and function.

In the creation, God ordained government as the means by which human beings and angelic hosts are ruled. The rest of the created order is governed by instinct (Prov. 30:24–28) and God's providence. Insect colonies, for example, may show a level of order, but this is due merely to genetically controlled instinct.

Human beings, on the other hand, are created in the image of God and thus are responsible to the commands of God. We are created by a God of order (1 Cor. 14:33); therefore we also seek order through governmental structures.

A Christian view of government differs significantly from views proposed by many political theorists. The basis for civil government is rooted in our created nature. We are rational and volitional beings. We are not determined by fate, as the Greeks would have said, nor are we determined by our environment as modern behaviorists say. We have the power of choice. Therefore we can exercise delegated power over the created order. Thus a biblical view of human nature requires a governmental system that acknowledges human responsibility.

While the source of civil government is rooted in human responsibility, the need for government derives from the necessity of controlling human sinfulness. God ordained civil government to restrain evil (cf. Gen. 9). Anarchy, for example, is not a viable option because all have sinned (Rom. 3:23) and are in need of external control.

A Christian view of human nature provides a basis to judge various political philosophies. For example, Christians must reject political philosophies, which ignore human sinfulness. Many utopian political theories are based on this flawed assumption.

In *The Republic*, Plato proposed an ideal government where the enlightened philosopher-kings would lead the country. The Bible, however, teaches that all are sinful (Rom. 3:23). Plato's proposed leaders would also be affected by the sinful effects of the Fall (Gen. 3). They would not always have the benevolent and enlightened disposition necessary to lead the republic.

Christians should also reject a Marxist view of government. Karl Marx believed that human nature was conditioned by society, and in particular, the capitalist economy. His solution was to change the economy so that you would change human nature. Why do we have greed? Because we live in a greedy capitalist society.

Marx taught that if society changed the economy from capitalism to socialism and then communism, greed would cease.

Christians should reject the utopian vision of Marxism because it is based upon an inaccurate view of human nature. The Bible teaches that believers can become new creatures (2 Cor. 5:17) through spiritual conversion, but that does not mean that the effects of sin are completely overcome in this life. The Bible also teaches that we will continue to live in a world tainted by sin. The view of Karl Marx contradicts biblical teaching by proposing a new man in a new society perfected by man's own efforts.

Since civil government is necessary and divinely ordained by God (Rom. 13:1–7), it is ultimately under God's control. It has been given three political responsibilities: the sword of justice (to punish criminals), the sword of order (to thwart rebellion), and the sword of war (to defend the state).

As citizens, Christians have been given a number of responsibilities. They are called to render service and obedience to the government (Matt. 22:21). Because it is a God-ordained institution, they are to submit to civil authority (1 Pet. 2:13–17) as they would to other institutions of God. As will be discussed later, Christians are not to give total and final allegiance to the secular state. Other God-ordained institutions exist in society alongside the state. Christians' final allegiance must be to God. They are to obey civil authorities (Rom.13:5) in order to avoid anarchy and chaos, but there may be times when they may be forced to disobey (Acts 5:29).

Because government is a divinely ordained institution, Christians have a responsibility to work within governmental structures to bring about change. Government is part of the order of creation and a minister of God (Rom. 13:4). Christians are to obey governmental authorities (Rom. 13:1–4, 1 Peter 2:13-14). Christians are also to be the salt of the earth and the light of the world (Matt. 5:13–16) in the midst of the political context.

Although governments may be guilty of injustice, Christians should not stop working for justice or cease to be concerned about human rights. We do not give up on marriage as an institution simply because there are so many divorces, and we do not give up on the church because of many internal problems. Each God-ordained institution manifests human sinfulness and disobedience. Our responsibility as Christians is to call political leaders back to this God-ordained task. Government is a legitimate sphere of Christian service, and so we should not look to government only when our rights are being abused. We are to be concerned with social justice and should see governmental action as a legitimate instrument to achieve just ends.

A Christian view of government should also be concerned with human rights. Human rights in a Christian system are based on a biblical view of human dignity. A bill of rights, therefore, does not grant rights to individuals but instead acknowledges these rights as already existing. The writings of John Locke along with the Declaration of Independence capture this idea by stating that government is based on the inalienable rights of individuals. Government based on humanism, however, would not see rights as inalienable, and thus opens the possibility for the state to redefine what rights its citizens may enjoy. The rights of citizens in a republic, for example, are articulated in terms of what the government is forbidden to do. But in totalitarian governments, while the rights of citizens may also be spelled out, power ultimately resides in the government, not the people.

A Christian view of government also recognizes the need to limit the influence of sin in society. This is best achieved by placing certain checks on governmental authority. This protects citizens from the abuse or misuse of governmental power which results when sinful individuals are given too much governmental control.

The greatest threat to liberty comes from the exercise of power. History has shown that power is a corrupting force when placed in human hands. In the Old Testament theocracy, there was less danger of abuse because the head of state was God. The Bible amply documents the dangers that ensued when power was transferred to a single king. Even David, a man after God's own heart (1 Sam. 13:14; Acts 13:22), abused his power and Israel experienced great calamity (2 Sam. 11–21).

Governmental Authority

A key question in political theory is how to determine the limits of governmental authority. With the remarkable growth in the size and scope of government in the last century, it is necessary to define clearly the lines of governmental authority. The Bible provides some guidelines.

However, it is often difficult to set limits or draw lines on governmental authority. As already noted, the Old Testament theocracy differed from our modern democratic government. Although human nature is the same, drawing biblical principles from an agrarian, monolithic culture and applying them to a technological, pluralistic culture requires discernment.

As Christians, we recognize that God has ordained other institutions besides civil government that exercises authority in their particular sphere of influence. This is in contrast to other political systems that see the state as the sovereign agent over human affairs, exercising sovereignty over every other human institution. A Christian view is different.

The first institution is the church (Heb. 12:18–24; 1 Pet. 2:9–10). Jesus taught that the government should work in harmony with the church and should recognize its sovereignty in spiritual matters (Matt. 22:21).

The second institution is the family (Eph. 5:22–32, 1 Pet. 3:1–7). The family is an institution under God and His authority (Gen.1:26–28, 2:20–25). When the family breaks down, the government often has to step in to protect the rights of the wife (in cases of wife abuse) or children (in cases of child abuse or adoption). The biblical emphasis, however, is not so much on rights as it is on responsibilities and mutual submission (Eph. 5:21).

A third institution is education. Children are not the wards of the state, but belong to God (Ps. 127:3) and are given to parents as a gift from God. Parents are to teach their children (Deut. 4:9) and may also entrust them to tutors (Gal. 4:2).

In a humanistic system of government, the institutions of church and family are usually subordinated to the state. In an atheistic system, ultimately the state becomes a substitute god and is given additional power to adjudicate disputes and bring order to a society. Since institutions exist by permission of the state, there is always the possibility that a new social contract will allow government to intervene in the areas of church and family.

A Christian view of government recognizes the sovereignty of these spheres.

Governmental intervention into the spheres of church and family is necessary in certain cases where there is a threat to life, liberty, or property. Otherwise, civil government should recognize the sovereignty of other God-ordained institutions.

Moral Basis of Law

Law should be the foundation of any government. Whether law is based upon moral absolutes, changing consensus or totalitarian whim is of crucial importance. Until fairly recently, Western culture held to a notion that common law was founded upon God's revealed moral absolutes.

In a Christian view of government, law is based upon God's revealed commandments. Law is not based upon human opinion or sociological convention. Law is rooted in God's unchangeable character and derived from biblical principles of morality.

In humanism, humanity is the source of law. Law is merely the expression of human will or mind. Since ethics and morality are man-made, so also is law. Humanists' law is rooted in human opinion, and thus is relative and arbitrary.

Two important figures in the history of law are Samuel Rutherford (1600-1661) and William Blackstone (1723-1780). Rutherford's *Lex Rex* (written in 1644) had profound effect on British and American law. His treatise challenged the foundations of 17th-century politics by proclaiming that law must be based upon the Bible, rather than upon the word of any man.

Up until that time, the king had been the law. The book created a great controversy because it attacked the idea of the divine right of kings. This doctrine had held that the king or the state ruled as God's appointed regent. Thus, the king's word had been law. Rutherford properly argued from passages such as Romans 13 that the king, as well as anyone else, was under God's law and not above it.

11

Sir William Blackstone was an English jurist in the 18th century and is famous for his *Commentaries on the Law of England*, which embodied the tenets of Judeo-Christian theism. Published in 1765, the *Commentaries* became the definitive treatise on the common law in England and in America. According to Blackstone, the two foundations for law are nature and revelation through the Scriptures. Blackstone believed that the fear of the Lord was the beginning of wisdom and thus taught that God was the source of all laws. It is interesting that even the humanist Rousseau noted in his *Social Contract* that one needs someone outside the world system to provide a moral basis for law. He said, "It would take gods to give men laws."

Unfortunately, our modern legal structure has been influenced by relativism and utilitarianism, instead of moral absolutes revealed in Scripture. Relativism provides no secure basis for moral judgments. There are no firm moral absolutes upon which to build a secure legal foundation.

Utilitarianism looks merely at consequences and ignores moral principles. This legal foundation has been further eroded by the relatively recent phenomenon of sociological law. In this view, law should be based upon relative sociological standards. No discipline is more helpless without a moral foundation than law. Law is a tool, and it needs a jurisprudential foundation. Just as contractors and builders need the architect's blueprint in order to build, so also lawyers need theologians and moral philosophers to make good laws. Yet, most lawyers today are extensively trained in technique, but little in moral and legal philosophy.

Legal justice in the Western world has been based on a proper, biblical understanding of human nature and human choice. We hold criminals accountable for their crimes, rather than excuse their behavior as part of environmental conditioning. We also acknowledge differences between willful, premeditated acts (such as murder) and so-called crimes of passion (i.e., manslaughter) or accidents.

One of the problems in our society today is that we do not operate from assumptions of human choice. The influence of the behaviorist, the evolutionist, and the sociobiologist are quite profound. The evolutionist and sociobiologist say that human behavior is genetically determined. The behaviorist says that human behavior is environmentally determined. Where do we find free choice in a system that argues that actions are a result of heredity and environment? Free choice and personal responsibility have been diminished in the criminal justice system, due to the influence of these secular perspectives.

It is, therefore, not by accident that we have seen a dramatic change in our view of criminal justice. The emphasis has moved from a view of punishment and restitution to one of rehabilitation. If our actions are governed by something external and human choice is denied, then we cannot punish someone for something they cannot control. However, we must rehabilitate them if the influences are merely heredity and environmental. But such a view of human actions diminishes human dignity. If a person cannot choose, then he is merely a victim of circumstances and must become a ward of the state.

As Christians, we must take the criminal act seriously and punish human choices. While we recognize the value of rehabilitation (especially through spiritual conversion, John 3:3), we also recognize the need for punishing wrong-doing. The Old Testament provisions for punishment and restitution make more sense in light of the biblical view of human nature.

CHAPTER 2 American Government and Christianity

America's Christian Roots

The founding of this country, as well as the framing of the key political documents, rests upon a Christian foundation. That doesn't necessarily mean that the United States is a Christian nation, although some framers used that term. But it does mean that the foundations of this republic presuppose a Christian view of human nature and God's providence.

The next chapter we look at the Christian roots of the Declaration and Constitution. The focus of this chapter is to pull together many of the themes of these resources and combine them with additional facts and quotes from the founders.

What was the perspective of the founders of America? Consider some of these famous quotes.

John Adams was the second president of the United States. He saw the need for religious values to provide the moral baseline for society. He stated in a letter to the officers of the First Brigade of the Third Division of the Militia of Massachusetts:

> We have no government armed with power capable of contending with human passions unbridled by morality and religion. Avarice, ambition, revenge, or gallantry, would break the strongest cords of our Constitution as a whale goes through a net. Our Constitution was made only for a moral and religious

people. It is wholly inadequate to the government of any other.[1]

In fact, John Adams was not the only founding father to talk about the importance of religious values. Consider this statement from George Washington during his Farewell Address:

> And let us with caution indulge the supposition, that morality can be maintained without religion. Whatever may be conceded to the influence of refined education on minds of peculiar structure, reason and experience both forbid us to expect that national morality can prevail in exclusion of religious principle.[2]

Two hundred years after the establishment of the Plymouth colony in 1620, Americans gathered at that site to celebrate its bicentennial. Daniel Webster was the speaker at this 1820 celebration. He reminded those in attendance of this nation's origins:

> Let us not forget the religious character of our origin. Our fathers were brought hither by their high veneration for the Christian religion. They journeyed by its light, and labored in its hope. They sought to incorporate its principles with the elements of their society, and to

---

[1] John Adams, October 11, 1798, in a letter to the officers of the First Brigade of the Third Division of the Militia of Massachusetts. Charles Francis Adams, ed., *The Works of John Adams – Second President of the United States: with a Life of the Author, Notes, and Illustration* (Boston: Little, Brown, & Co., 1854), Vol. IX, 228-229.

[2] George Washington, Farewell Address (September 19, 1796). Address of George Washington, President of the United States, and Late Commander in Chief of the American Army. To the People of the United States, Preparatory to His Declination.

diffuse its influence through all their institutions, civil, political, or literary.[3]

Religion, and especially the Christian religion, was an important foundation of this republic.

Christian Character

It is clear that the framers of this new government believed that the people should elect and support leaders with character and integrity. George Washington expressed this in his Farewell Address when he said, "Of all the dispositions and habits which lead to political prosperity, Religion and Morality are indispensable supports."

Benjamin Rush talked about the religious foundation of the republic that demanded virtuous leadership. He said that "the only foundation for a useful education in a republic is to be laid on the foundation of religion. Without this, there can be no virtue, and without virtue, there can be no liberty, and liberty is the object and life of all republican governments."[4]

He went on to explain that:

> A Christian cannot fail of being a republican . . . for every precept of the Gospel inculcates those degrees of humility, self- denial, and brotherly kindness which are directly opposed to the pride of monarchy. . . . A Christian cannot fail of being useful to the republic, for his religion teaches him that no

---

[3] Daniel Webster, December 22, 1820. *The Works of Daniel Webster* (Boston: Little, Brown and Company, 1853), Vol. I, 48.

[4] Benjamin Rush, "Thoughts upon the Mode of Education Proper in a Republic," Early American Imprints. *Benjamin Rush, Essays, Literary, Moral and Philosophical* (Philadelphia: Thomas and Samuel F. Bradford, 1798), 8.

man "liveth to himself." And lastly a Christian cannot fail of being wholly inoffensive, for his religion teaches him in all things to do to others what he would wish, in like circumstances, they should do to him.[5]

Daniel Webster understood the importance of religion, and especially the Christian religion, in this form of government. In his famous Plymouth Rock speech of 1820 he said,

> Lastly, our ancestors established their system of government on morality and religious sentiment. Moral habits, they believed, cannot safely be trusted on any other foundation than religious principle, nor any government be secure which is not supported by moral habits. . . .Whatever makes men good Christians, makes them good citizens.[6]

John Jay was one of the authors of the Federalist Papers and became America's first Supreme Court Justice. He also served as the president of the American Bible Society. He understood the relationship between government and Christian values. He said, "Providence has given to our people the choice of their rulers, and it is the duty, as well as the privilege and interest of our Christian nation to select and prefer Christians for their rulers."[7]

William Penn writing the *Frame of Government* for his new colony said, "Government, like clocks, go from the motion men give them; and as governments are

---

[5] Ibid.

[6] Webster, *The Works of Daniel Webster*, 22ff.

[7] John Jay, October 12, 1816, in *The Correspondence and Public Papers of John Jay*, Henry P. Johnston, ed., (New York: G.P Putnam & Sons, 1893; reprinted NY: Burt Franklin, 1970), Vol. IV, 393.

made and moved by men, so by them they are ruined too. Wherefore governments rather depend upon men, than men upon governments. Let men be good, and the government cannot be bad."[8] The founders believed that good character was vital to the health of the nation.

New Man

Historian C. Gregg Singer traces the line of influence from the seventeenth century to the eighteenth century in his book, *A Theological Interpretation of American History*. He says,

Whether we look at the Puritans and their fellow colonists of the seventeenth century, or their descendants of the eighteenth century, or those who framed the Declaration of Independence and the Constitution, we see that their political programs were the rather clear reflection of a consciously held political philosophy, and that the various political philosophies which emerged among the American people were intimately related to the theological developments which were taking place. . . . A Christian world and life view furnished the basis for this early political thought which guided the American people for nearly two centuries and whose crowning lay in the writing of the Constitution of 1787.[9]

Actually, the line of influence extends back even further. Historian Arnold Toynbee, for example, has written that the American Revolution was made possible by American Protestantism. Page Smith, writing in

---

[8] William Penn, April 25, 1682, in the preface of his Frame of Government of Pennsylvania. A Collection of Charters and Other Public Acts Relating to the Province of Pennsylvania (Philadelphia: B. Franklin, 1740), 10-12.

[9] C. Gregg Singer, *A Theological Interpretation of American History* (Nutley, NJ: The Craig Press, 1964), 284-5.

the *Religious Origins of the American Revolution*, cites the influence of the Protestant Reformation. He believes that

> The Protestant Reformation produced a new kind of consciousness and a new kind of man. The English Colonies in America, in turn, produced a new unique strain of that consciousness. It thus follows that it is impossible to understand the intellectual and moral forces behind the American Revolution without understanding the role that Protestant Christianity played in shaping the ideals, principles and institutions of colonial America.[10]

Smith argues that the American Revolution "started, in a sense, when Martin Luther nailed his 95 theses to the church door at Wittenburg." It received "its theological and philosophical underpinnings from John Calvin's *Institutes of the Christian Religion* and much of its social theory from the Puritan Revolution of 1640-1660.[11]

Most people before the Reformation belonged to classes and social groups which set the boundaries of their worlds and established their identities. The Reformation, according to Smith, changed these perceptions. Luther and Calvin, in a sense, created a reformed individual in a reformed world.

Key to this is the doctrine of the priesthood of the believer where each person is "responsible directly to God for his or her own spiritual state…. The individuals who formed the new congregations established their own churches chose their own ministers, and managed their

---

[10] Page Smith, *Religious Origins of the American Revolution* (Missoula, MT: Scholars Press, 1976), 1.

[11] Ibid., 2.

own affairs without reference to an ecclesiastical hierarchy."[12]

These re-formed individuals began to change their world including their view of government and authority.

Declaration of Independence

Was there any Christian influence on the Declaration of Independence? Historian Page Smith points out that Thomas Jefferson was not only influenced by secular philosophers but was also influenced by the Protestant Reformation. He says,

> Jefferson and other secular-minded Americans subscribed to certain propositions about law and authority that had their roots in the Protestant Reformation. It is a scholarly common-place to point out how much Jefferson (and his fellow delegates to the Continental Congress) were influenced by Locke. Without disputing this we would simply add that an older and deeper influence — John Calvin — was of more profound importance.[13]

Another important influence was William Blackstone. Jefferson drew heavily on the writings of this highly respected jurist. In fact, Blackstone's *Commentaries on the Laws of England* were among Jefferson's most favorite books.

In his section on the "Nature of Laws in General," Blackstone wrote, "as man depends absolutely upon his Maker for everything, it is necessary that he should, in all

---

[12] Ibid., 3.

[13] Ibid., 185.

points, conform to his Maker's will. This will of his Maker is called the law of nature."[14]

In addition to the law of nature, the other source of law is from divine revelation. "The doctrines thus delivered we call the revealed or divine law, and they are to be found only in the Holy Scriptures." According to Blackstone, all human laws depended either upon the law of nature or upon the law of revelation found in the Bible: "Upon these two foundations, the law of nature and the law of revelation, depend all human laws."[15]

Samuel Adams argues in "The Rights of the Colonists" that they had certain rights. "Among the natural Rights of the Colonists are these: First, a Right to Life; second, to Liberty; third, to Property; . . . and in the case of intolerable oppression, civil or religious, to leave the society they belong to, and enter into another. When men enter into society, it is by voluntary consent."[16] This concept of natural rights also found its way into the Declaration of Independence and provided the justification for the American Revolution.

The Declaration was a bold document, but not a radical one. The colonists did not break with England for "light and transient causes." They were mindful that they should be "in subjection to governing authorities" which "are established by God" (Rom. 13:1). Yet when they suffered from a "long train of abuses and usurpations," they believed that "it is the right of the people to alter or abolish [the existing government] and to institute a new government."

---

[14] William Blackstone, "Of the Nature of Laws in General," *Commentaries on the Laws of England*, Book 1, Section II.

[15] Ibid.

[16] Samuel Adams, "The Rights of the Colonists" (Boston, 1772), The Annals of America, Vol. II, 217.

Constitution

Was there any Christian influence on the Constitution? James Madison was the chief architect of the Constitution as well as one of the authors of the *Federalist Papers*. It is important to note that as a youth, he studied under a Scottish Presbyterian, Donald Robertson. Madison gave the credit to Robertson for "all that I have been in life."[17] Later he was trained in theology at Princeton under the Reverend John Witherspoon. Scholars believe that Witherspoon's Calvinism (which emphasized the fallen nature of man) was an important source for Madison's political ideas.[18]

The Constitution was a contract between the people and had its origins in American history a century earlier:

> One of the obvious by-products [of the Reformation] was the notion of a contract entered into by two people or by the members of a community amongst themselves that needed no legal sanctions to make it binding. This concept of the Reformers made possible the formation of contractuals or, as the Puritans called them, "covenanted" groups formed by individuals who signed a covenant or agreement to found a community. The most famous of these covenants was the Mayflower Compact. In it the Pilgrims formed a "civil body politic," and promised to obey the laws their own government might pass. In short, the individual Pilgrim invented on the spot a new

---

[17] John Eidsmoe, *Christianity and the Constitution* (Grand Rapids, MI: Baker Books, 1987), 94.

[18] James H. Smylie, "Madison and Witherspoon: Theological Roots of American Political Thought," *American Presbyterians*

community, one that would be ruled by laws of its making.[19]

Historian Page Smith believes, "The Federal Constitution was in this sense a monument to the reformed consciousness. This new sense of time as potentiality was a vital element in the new consciousness that was to make a revolution and, what was a good deal more difficult, form a new nation."[20]

Preaching and teaching within the churches provided the justification for the revolution and the establishment of a new nation. Alice Baldwin, writing in *The New England Clergy and the American Revolution*, says,

> The teachings of the New England ministers provide one line of unbroken descent. For two generations and more New Englanders had . . . been taught that these rights were sacred and came from God and that to preserve them they had a legal right of resistance and, if necessary a right to . . . alter and abolish governments and by common consent establish new ones.[21]

Christian ideas were important in the founding of this republic and the framing of our American governmental institutions. Moreover, I believe they are equally important in the maintenance of that republic.

---

[19] *Smith, Religious Origins.*

[20] Ibid., 4.

[21] Alice M. Baldwin, *The New England Clergy and the American Revolution* (Durham: Duke University Press, 1928), 169.

SECTION 2 Founding Principles

CHAPTER 3 Declaration and Constitution: Their Christian Roots

The Declaration of Independence

Many are unaware of the writings and documents that preceded these great works and the influence of biblical ideas in their formation. In the first two sections of this chapter, we will examine the Declaration of Independence. Following this, we will look at the Constitution.

On June 7, 1776, Richard Henry Lee introduced a resolution to the Continental Congress calling for a formal declaration of independence. However, even at that late date, there was significant opposition to the resolution. So, Congress recessed for three weeks to allow delegates to return home and discuss the proposition with their constituents while a committee was appointed to express the Congressional sentiments. The task of composing the Declaration fell to Thomas Jefferson.

Jefferson's initial draft left God out of the manuscript entirely except for a vague reference to "the laws of nature and of nature's God." Yet, even this phrase makes an implicit reference to the laws of God.

The phrase "laws of nature" had a fixed meaning in 18th century England and America. It was a direct reference to the laws of God in a created order as described in John Locke's *Second Treatise on Civil Government* and William Blackstone's *Commentaries on the Laws of England*.

What Jefferson was content to leave implicit, however, was made more explicit by the other members of the committee. They changed the language to read that all men are "endowed by their Creator" with these rights. Later, the Continental Congress added phrases, which further reflected a theistic perspective. For example, they added that they were "appealing to the Supreme Judge of the World for the rectitude of our intentions" and that they were placing "firm reliance on the protection of divine Providence."

The Declaration was not drafted in an intellectual vacuum, nor did the ideas contained in it suddenly spring from the minds of a few men. Instead, the founders built their framework upon a Reformation foundation laid by such men as Samuel Rutherford and later incorporated by John Locke.

Rutherford wrote his book *Lex Rex* in 1644 to refute the idea of the divine right of kings. *Lex Rex* established two crucial principles. First, there should be a covenant or constitution between the ruler and the people. Second, since all men are sinners, no man is superior to another. These twin principles of liberty and equality are also found in John Locke's writings.

John Locke and the Origin of the Declaration

Although the phrasing of the Declaration certainly follows the pattern of John Locke, Jefferson also gave credit to the writer Algernon Sidney, who in turn cites most prominently Aristotle, Plato, Roman republican writers, and the Old Testament.

Legal scholar Gary Amos argues that Locke's *Two Treatises on Government* is simply Samuel Rutherford's *Lex Rex* in a popularized form. Amos says in his book *Defending the Declaration*,

> Locke explained that the "law of nature" is God's general revelation of law in creation, which God also supernaturally writes on the

hearts of men. Locke drew the idea from the New Testament in Romans 1 and 2. In contrast, he spoke of the "law of God" or the "positive law of God" as God's eternal moral law specially revealed and published in Scripture.[22]

This foundation helps explain the tempered nature of the American Revolution. The Declaration of Independence was a bold document, but not a radical one. The colonists did not break with England for "light and transient causes." They were mindful that they should be "in subjection to the governing authorities" which "are established by God" (Romans 13:1). Yet when they suffered from a "long train of abuses and usurpations," they argued, "It is the right of the people to alter or to abolish it, and to institute a new government."

The Declaration also borrowed from state constitutions that already existed at the time. In fact, the phraseology of the Declaration greatly resembles the preamble to the Virginia Constitution, adopted in June 1776. The body of the Declaration consists of twenty-eight charges against the king justifying the break with Britain. All but four are from state constitutions.[23]

Jefferson no doubt drew from George Mason's Declaration of Rights (published on June 6, 1776). The first paragraph states that "all men are born equally free and independent and have certain inherent natural Rights; among which are the Enjoyment of Life and Liberty, with the Means of Acquiring and possessing property, and pursuing and obtaining Happiness and Safety." Mason also argued that when any government is

---

[22] Gary Amos, *Defending the Declaration* (Brentwood, TN: Wolgemuth and Hyatt, 1989), 57.

[23] Donald S. Lutz, *The Origins of American Constitutionalism* (Baton Rouge: Louisiana State University Press, 1988, 114.

found unworthy of the trust placed in it, a majority of the community "hath an indubitable, inalienable, and indefensible Right to Reform, alter, or abolish it."

Constitution and Human Nature

The influence of the Bible on the Constitution was profound but often not appreciated by secular historians and political theorists. Two decades ago, Constitutional scholars and political historians (including one of my professors at Georgetown University) assembled 15,000 writings from the Founding Era (1760-1805). They counted 3154 citations in these writings and found that the book most frequently cited in that literature was the Bible. The writers from the Foundering Era quoted from the Bible 34 percent of the time. Even more interesting was that about three-fourths of all references to the Bible came from reprinted sermons from that era.[24]

Professor M.E. Bradford shows in his book, *A Worthy Company*, that fifty of the fifty-five men who signed the Constitution were church members who endorsed the Christian faith.[25]

The Bible and biblical principles were important in the framing of the Constitution. In particular, the framers started with a biblical view of human nature. James Madison argued in *Federalist #51* that government must be based upon a realistic view of human nature.

> But what is government itself but the greatest of all reflections on human nature? If men were angels, no government would be necessary. If angels were to govern men,

---

[24] Ibid., 140.

[25] M.E. Bradford, *A Worthy Company: Brief Lives of the Framers of the United States Constitution* (Marlborough, NH: Plymouth Rock Foundation, 1982).

neither external nor internal controls on government would be necessary. In framing a government which is to be administered by men over men, the great difficulty lies in this: you must first enable the government to control the governed; and in the next place oblige it to control itself.[26]

Framing a republic requires a balance of power that liberates human dignity and rationality and controls human sin and depravity.

As there is a degree of depravity in mankind which requires a certain degree of circumspection and distrust, so there are other qualities in human nature, which justify a certain portion of esteem and confidence. Republican government presupposes the existence of these qualities in a higher degree than any other form.[27]

A Christian view of government is based upon a balanced view of human nature. It recognizes both human dignity (we are created in God's image) and human depravity (we are sinful individuals). Because both grace and sin operate in government, we should neither be too optimistic nor too pessimistic. Instead, the framers constructed a government with a deep sense of biblical realism.

Constitution and Majority Tyranny

James Madison in defending the Constitution divided the problem of tyranny into two broad categories: majority tyranny (addressed in *Federalist* #10)

---

[26] James Madison, *Federalist*, #51 (New York: New American Library, 1961), 322.

[27] Ibid., *Federalist* #55, 346.

and governmental tyranny (addressed in *Federalist* #47-51).

Madison concluded from his study of governments that factions destroyed them. He believed this factionalism was due to "the propensity of mankind, to fall into mutual animosities" (*Federalist* #10) which he believed were "sown in the nature of man." Government, he concluded, must be based upon a more realistic view, which also accounts for this sinful side of human nature.

A year before the Constitutional Convention, George Washington wrote to John Jay that, "We have, probably, had too good an opinion of human nature in forming our federation." From now on, he added, "We must take human nature as we find it."

Madison's solution to majority tyranny was the term *extended republic*. His term for the solution to governmental tyranny was *compound republic*. He believed that an extended republic with a greater number of citizens would prevent factions from easily taking control of government. He also believed that elections would serve to filter upward men of greater virtue.

Madison's solution to governmental tyranny can be found in *Federalist* #47-51. These include separation of powers, checks and balances, and federalism.

Madison realized the futility of trying to remove passions (human sinfulness) from the population. Therefore, he proposed that human nature be set against human nature. This was done by separating various institutional power structures. First, the church was separated from the state so that ecclesiastical functions and governmental functions would not interfere with religious and political liberty. Second, the federal government was divided into three equal branches: executive, legislative, and judicial. Third, the federal government was delegated certain powers while the rest of the powers resided in the state governments.

Each branch was given separate but rival powers, thus preventing the possibility of concentrating power into the hands of a few. Each branch had certain checks over the other branches so that there was a distribution and balance of power. The effect of this system was to allow ambition and power to control itself. As each branch is given power, it provides a check on the other branch. This what has often been referred to as the concept of "countervailing ambitions."

Constitution and Governmental Tyranny

James Madison's solution to governmental tyranny includes both federalism as well as the separation of powers. Federalism can be found at the very heart of the United States Constitution. In fact, without federalism, there was no practical reason for the framers to abandon the Articles of Confederation and draft the Constitution.

Federalism comes from *foedus*, Latin for covenant. "The tribes of Israel shared a covenant that made them a nation. American federalism originated at least in part in the dissenting Protestants' familiarity with the Bible."[28]

The separation of powers allows each branch of government to provide a check on the other. According to Madison, the Constitution provides a framework of supplying "opposite and rival interests" (*Federalist #*51) through a series of checks and balances. This theory of "countervailing ambition" both prevented tyranny and provided liberty. It was a system in which bad people could do least harm and good people had the freedom to do good works.

---

[28] Lutz, *Origins*, 43.

31

For example, the executive branch cannot take over the government and rule at its whim because the legislative branch has been given the power of the purse. Congress must approve or disapprove budgets for governmental programs. A President cannot wage war if the Congress does not appropriate money for its execution.

Likewise, the legislative branch is also controlled by this structure of government. It can pass legislation, but it always faces the threat of a presidential veto and judicial oversight. Since the executive branch is responsible for the execution of legislation, the legislature cannot exercise complete control over the government. Undergirding all of this is the authority of the ballot box.

Each of these checks was motivated by a healthy fear of human nature. The founders believed in human responsibility and human dignity, but they did not trust human nature too much. Their solution was to separate powers and invest each branch with rival powers.

Biblical ideas were crucial in both the Declaration and the Constitution. Nearly 80 percent of the political pamphlets published during the 1770s were reprinted sermons. As one political science professor put it: "When reading comprehensively in the political literature of the war years, one cannot but be struck by the extent to which biblical sources used by ministers and traditional Whigs undergirded the justification for the break with Britain, the rationale for continuing the war, and the basic principles of Americans' writing their own constitutions."[29]

---

[29] Ibid., 142.

CHAPTER 4 Bill of Rights

The Bill of Rights is the first ten amendments to the Constitution. It establishes the basic civil liberties that the federal government cannot violate.

When the Constitution was drafted, some were fearful that a federal government would usurp the rights and powers of the states and the people. Critics were fearful that the federal government would exceed its enumerated powers—a fear that in hindsight seems most reasonable. The Bill of Rights was designed to address those apprehensions. The states ratified the Bill of Rights in 1791, three years after the Constitution was ratified.[30]

First Amendment

Congress shall make no law respecting an establishment of religion, or prohibiting the free exercise thereof; or abridging the freedom of speech, or of the press, or the right of the people peaceably to assemble, and to petition the Government for a redress of grievances.

The First Amendment begins by preventing Congress from establishing religion or prohibiting the free exercise of religion. Originally, the religion clause of the First Amendment was intended to prevent the federal government from establishing a national church. Some New England states maintained established state churches until the 1830s.

In the last century, the Supreme Court has extended the First Amendment to any religious activity by any

---

[30] A longer summary of the Bill of Rights can be found in David M. Wagner, *Freedom Forum: A Commentary on the Bill of Rights*, Washington, DC: Family Research Council, 2000.

governmental body. The establishment clause originally prohibited the establishment of a national church by Congress, but now has been broadened to prohibit anything that appears like a government endorsement of religious practice. The free exercise clause supposedly prohibits government from placing any burden on religious practice.

The second part of the First Amendment provides freedom of political participation. This includes freedom of speech, freedom of the press, and freedom of assembly with the right to petition the government for a redress of grievances. This quartet of freedoms allows citizens to be actively involved in electing representatives and influencing legislation.

Second Amendment

A well regulated Militia, being necessary to the security of a free State, the right of the people to keep and bear Arms, shall not be infringed.

The Second Amendment gives Americans the right to keep and bear arms. Although the amendment clearly provides such rights, proponents of limiting a citizen's right to arms attempt to argue that the amendment only applies to a militia like the National Guard.

Before the drafting of the Constitution, citizen-militias existed to guarantee order and domestic security. The framers envisioned an armed citizenry that was separate from a federal military that could be controlled by government authorities. They were well aware of the abuses that came when a King or Prime Minister could control a standing army. Armed citizens provided an important check and balance of power. The framers well understood the threat to freedom when gun ownership was a government monopoly.

Third Amendment

No Soldier shall, in time of peace, be quartered in any house, without the consent of the Owner, nor in time of war, but in a manner to be prescribed by law.

The Third Amendment guarantees that no soldier may be quartered in any house without the consent of the owner. At its face, this would seem to be an obsolete amendment since the federal government has never placed soldiers in private homes.

Unfortunately, this amendment has been used to make the case for a right to privacy in the U.S. Constitution. The Supreme Court cited this amendment in 1965 in the case of *Griswold v. Connecticut* involving the issue of contraceptives. This case provided the foundation for the infamous abortion case of *Roe v. Wade* in 1973.

Many legal scholars question whether the Constitution has an implicit right to privacy. Obviously, the Third Amendment provides homeowners with protection against unreasonable military intrusion. But it is quite a stretch to manipulate this amendment into a justification for a right to privacy with regard to contraception or abortion.

Fourth Amendment

The right of the people to be secure in their persons, houses, papers, and effects, against unreasonable searches and seizures, shall not be violated, and no Warrants shall issue, but upon probable cause, supported by Oath or affirmation, and particularly describing the place to be searched, and the persons or things to be seized.

The Fourth Amendment requires that a specific warrant be obtained before a search is made of a person, their house, their papers, or personal effects. The framers wanted to ban the British practice of obtaining a general warrant, which allowed the seizure of anything in the suspect's home. A search requires a specific warrant issued by a neutral magistrate.

In the last century, the Supreme Court has refined the amendment through what is called "the exclusionary rule." Evidence obtained outside the specific requirements of the warrant is inadmissible in a court of law. Cases in court often swing on whether evidence was obtained legally and whether the law enforcement officer acted in "good faith" in the securing of that evidence.

Fifth Amendment

No person shall be held to answer for a capital, or otherwise infamous crime, unless on a presentment or indictment of a Grand Jury, except in cases arising in the land or naval forces, or in the Militia, when in actual service in time of War or public danger; nor shall any person be subject for the same offence to be twice put in jeopardy of life or limb; nor shall be compelled in any criminal case to be a witness against himself, nor be deprived of life, liberty, or property, without due process of law; nor shall private property be taken for public use, without just compensation.

The Fifth Amendment is best known for guaranteeing a citizen's right to refrain from answering a question that might be incriminating. Actually, there is more to this amendment than "taking the fifth." The amendment also provides for due process, a grand jury, and freedom from double jeopardy.

Many citizens believe that the amendment guarantees your right to remain silent. Actually the amendment states that no person should be compelled to be a witness against himself. The right to remain silent comes from the so-called Miranda warnings read by a police officer before questioning. The Supreme Court mandated these phrases in an attempt to further protect the rights of the accused.

Sixth Amendment

In all criminal prosecutions, the accused shall enjoy the right to a speedy and public trial, by an impartial jury of the State and district wherein the crime shall have been committed, which district shall have been previously ascertained by law, and to be informed of the nature and cause of the accusation; to be confronted with the witnesses against him; to have compulsory process for obtaining witnesses in his favor, and to have the Assistance of Counsel for his defense.

The Sixth Amendment provides additional rights in a criminal trial. These include the right to an attorney, the right to a trial by jury, and the right to confront one's accusers.

The right to an attorney implies the right to "competent" counsel. Appeal courts have had to decide what constitutes competent or incompetent counsel. Usually a guilty verdict is allowed to stand if it seems that an attorney's actions did not significantly affect the judicial outcome.

The right to confront your accusers was a deliberate attempt to prevent the possibility of the U.S. some day having a Star Chamber as occurred previously in England. Witnesses must testify in open court and thus are available for cross-examination. The only cases where this is not done are in child abuse cases where child-victim testimony is allowed by videotape.

Seventh Amendment

In Suits at common law, where the value in controversy shall exceed twenty dollars, the right of trial by jury shall be preserved, and no fact tried by a jury, shall be otherwise re-examined in any Court of the United States, than according to the rules of the common law.

The Seventh Amendment addresses civil cases. It provides for a jury trial (in cases involving more than $20) that involves suits at common law. Although this seems like a logical right that would already be assumed, it reflects the concerns of the framers that a federal judiciary would set aside jury verdicts and perhaps even eliminate juries altogether.

Eighth Amendment

Excessive bail shall not be required, nor excessive fines imposed, nor cruel and unusual punishments inflicted.

The Eighth Amendment protects citizens against excessive actions. These include excessive bail, excessive fines, and cruel and unusual punishment. These were all provisions found in English law used to restrict the excesses of the English kings.

The Supreme Court on many occasions has been called upon to consider whether a particular punishment was proportional to the crime. This has also included a number of controversial rulings over the last few decades about whether long prison terms or capital punishment constitutes cruel and unusual punishment.

Ninth Amendment

The enumeration in the Constitution, of certain rights, shall not be construed to deny or disparage others retained by the people.

The Ninth Amendment prevents the courts from thinking that the rights listed in the first eight amendments are exclusive and exhaustive. In other words, just because the Constitution does not specifically list a right does not mean that right is not retained by the people.

Judicial activists have used this amendment to justify their expansion of additional rights. The Supreme Court reasoned in this way concerning the so-called right to privacy. The Court argued that the First, Third, Fourth, and Fifth Amendments all protect privacy in some way. Therefore, they argued that the right to privacy does exist and should be protected by the Constitution.

Tenth Amendment

The powers not delegated to the United States by the Constitution, nor prohibited by it to the States, are reserved to the States respectively, or to the people.

The Tenth Amendment protects the structure of federalism. Those powers not specifically delegated to the federal government are reserved to the States or the people. The framers intended that the people and the states would decide how power was to be delegated to the other levels of government (cities, towns, counties, etc.).

The Tenth Amendment was written to provide additional protection for federalism since many citizens were concerned with giving a national government too much power. Although the Tenth Amendment did provide some protection, its impact was undercut by the Fourteenth Amendment. That effectively made the federal government the ultimate protector of state's rights and has lessened its importance.

CHAPTER 5 The Federalist Papers

The Federalist Papers are a collection of eighty-five essays written by James Madison, Alexander Hamilton, and John Jay between October 1787 and May 1788. They were written at the time to convince New York State to ratify the U.S. Constitution.

They are perhaps the most famous newspaper columns ever written, and today constitute one of the most important documents of America's founding period. They provide the justification for the Constitution and address some of the most important political issues associated with popular self-government.

Clinton Rossiter says, "*The Federalist* is the most important work in political science that has ever been written, or is likely ever to be written, in the United States. . . . It would not be stretching the truth more than a few inches to say that *The Federalist* stands third only to the Declaration of Independence and the Constitution itself among all the sacred writings of American political history."[31] Jacob Cooke agrees. He believes that "The United States has produced three historic documents of major importance: The Declaration of Independence, the Constitution, and *The Federalist*."[32]

All the essays were signed "Publius" even though they were written by three different authors (Hamilton wrote fifty-two, Madison wrote twenty-eight, and Jay wrote five). Political leaders in New York opposed the new government because the state had become an independent nation under the Articles of Confederation

---

[31] Clinton Rossiter, *The Federalist Papers* (New York: New American Library, 1961), vii.

[32] Jacob E. Cooke, *The Federalist* (Middletown, CT: Wesleyan University Press, 1961), ix.

and was becoming rich through tariffs on trade with other states. When it became apparent that New York would not ratify the Constitution, Alexander Hamilton enlisted the aid of James Madison (who was available because the Continental Congress was sitting in New York) and John Jay. Unfortunately, Jay was injured and was only able to complete a few essays.

The Importance of the Federalist Papers

There are many reasons for the importance of *The Federalist Papers*. First, the authors were significant figures during the founding era. James Madison is considered the architect of the Constitution and later served as President of the United States. Alexander Hamilton served in George Washington's cabinet and was a major force in setting U.S. economic policy. John Jay became the first Chief Justice of the U.S. Supreme Court. Each of these men was present at the constitutional convention and was respected by their peers.

Second, *The Federalist Papers* provide the most systematic and comprehensive analysis of the constitution. Not only do the authors explain the structure of the constitution, but they also defend their decisions against the critics of their day. They were, after all, writing to convince New York to ratify the constitution.

Third, *The Federalist Papers* explain the motives of the Founding Fathers. Often when Supreme Court justices are trying to discern the founder's intentions, they appeal to these writings.[33] *The Federalist Papers* are the most

---

[33] James G. Wilson, "The Most Sacred Text: The Supreme Court's Use of The Federalist Papers," *Brigham Young University Law Review* 1 (1985).

important interpretative source of constitutional interpretation and give important insight into the framers' intent and purpose for the Constitution.

Human Nature

The writers of *The Federalist Papers* were concerned about the relationship between popular government and human nature. They were well aware that human beings have the propensity to pursue short-term self-interest often at the expense of long-term benefits. The writers were also concerned that factions that formed around these areas of immediate self-interest could ultimately destroy the moral foundations of civil government.

James Madison argued in *Federalist Paper #51* that government must be based upon a realistic view of human nature:

> But what is government itself but the greatest of all reflections on human nature? If men were angels, no government would be necessary. If angels were to govern men, neither external nor internal controls on government would be necessary. In framing a government which is to be administered by men over men, the great difficulty lies in this: you must first enable the government to control the governed; and in the next place oblige it to control itself.[34]

The writers of *The Federalist Papers* certainly believed that there was a positive aspect to human nature. They often talk about reason, virtue, and morality. However, they also recognized there was a negative aspect to human nature. They believed that

---

[34] James Madison, *Federalist Papers*, #51 (New York: New American Library, 1961), 322.

framing a republic required a balance of power that liberates human dignity and rationality and controls human sin and depravity.

> As there is a degree of depravity in mankind which requires a certain degree of circumspection and distrust, so there are other qualities in human nature which justify a certain portion of esteem and confidence. Republican government presupposes the existence of these qualities in a higher degree than any other form.[35]

As we will discuss in more detail later, James Madison concluded from his study of governments that they were destroyed by factions. He believed this factionalism was due to "the propensity of mankind, to fall into mutual animosities" (*Federalist Paper #10*) which he believed were "sown in the nature of man." Constitutional scholars have concluded that "the fallen nature of man influenced Madison's view of law and government."[36] He therefore concluded that government must be based upon a more realistic view, which also accounts for this sinful side of human nature.

A Christian view of government is based upon a balanced view of human nature. It recognizes both human dignity (we are created in God's image) and human depravity (we are sinful individuals). Because both grace and sin operate in government, we should neither be too optimistic nor too pessimistic. We should view governmental affairs with a deep sense of biblical realism.

---

[35] Madison, *Federalist Papers #55*, 346.

[36] John Eidsmoe, *Christianity and the Constitution* (Grand Rapids, MI: Baker Books, 1987), 101.

Factions and the Republic

The writers of *The Federalist Papers* were concerned about the previous history of republics. Alexander Hamilton writes that "the history of the petty republics of Greece and Italy" can only evoke "horror and disgust" since they rocked back and forth from "the extremes of tyranny and anarchy."

James Madison focused on the problem of factions. "By a faction I understand a number of citizens, whether amounting to a majority or minority of the whole, who are united and actuated by some common impulse of passion, or of interest, adverse to the rights of the citizens, or to the permanent and aggregate interests of the community."[37]

Madison believed there were only two ways to cure the problem of factions: remove the causes or control the effects. He quickly dismisses the first since it would either destroy liberty or require everyone to have "the same opinions, the same passions, and the same interests."

He further acknowledges that "causes of faction are thus sown in the nature of man." So he rejects the idea of changing human nature. And he also rejects the idea that a political leader will be able to deal with the problem of factions: "It is vain to say that enlightened statesmen will be able to adjust these clashing interests and render them all subservient to the public good. Enlightened statesmen will not always be at the helm."[38]

Madison believed the solution could be found in the extended republic that the framers created. While a small republic might be shattered by factions, the larger

---

[37] Madison, *The Federalist Papers*, #10, 78.

[38] Ibid., 80.

number of representatives that would be chosen would "guard against the cabals of a few."

Also, since "each representative will be chosen by a greater number of citizens, it will be more difficult for unworthy candidates to practice with success the vicious arts by which elections are too often carried." Also, the voters are "more likely to center on men who possess the most attractive merit and the most diffusive and established characters."[39]

Madison also believed that this extended republic would minimize the possibility of one faction pushing forward it agenda to the exclusion of others. This was due to the "greater number of citizens and extent of territory." A smaller society would most likely have fewer distinct parties. But if you extend the sphere, you increase the variety and interests of the parties. And it is less likely any one faction could dominate the political arena.

Madison realized the futility of trying to remove passions or human sinfulness, and instead designed a system that minimized the influence of factions and still provided the greatest amount of liberty for its citizens.

Separation of Powers

The writers of *The Federalist Papers* were concerned with the potential abuse of power and set forth their rationale for separating the powers of the various branches of government. James Madison summarizes their fear of the centralization of political power in a famous quote in *Federalist Paper #47*.

No political truth is certainly of greater intrinsic value or is stamped with the authority of more enlightened patrons of liberty, than that on which the

---

[39] Ibid., 82-3.

objection is founded. The accumulation of all powers, legislative, executive, and judiciary, in the same hands, whether of one, a few or many, and whether hereditary, self-appointed or elective, may justly be pronounced the very definition of tyranny.[40]

Madison quickly dismisses the idea that constitutional provisions alone will prevent an abuse of political power. He argues that mere "parchment barriers" are not adequate "against the encroaching spirit of power."[41]

He also believed that the legislature posed the greatest threat to the separation of powers. "The legislative department is everywhere extending the sphere of its activity and drawing all power into its impetuous vortex."[42] The framers, therefore, divided Congress into a bicameral legislature and hoped that the Senate would play a role in checking the passions of popular majorities (*Federalist Paper #63*).

His solution was to give each branch separate but rival powers. This prevented the possibility of concentrating power into the hands of a few. Each branch had certain checks over the other branches, so there were a distribution and balance of power.

The effect of this system was to allow ambition and power to control itself. Each branch is given power, and as ambitious men and women seek to extend their sphere of influence, they provide a check on the other branch.

Madison said, "Ambition must be made to counteract ambition. The interest of the man must be connected with the constitutional rights of the place. It may be a reflection on human nature that such devices

---

[40] Madison, *The Federalist Papers*, #47, 301.

[41] Madison, *The Federalist Papers*, #48, 308.

[42] Ibid., 309.

should be necessary to control the abuses of government."[43] This policy of supplying "opposite and rival interests" has been known as the concept of countervailing ambitions.

In addition to this, the people were given certain means of redress. Elections and an amendment process have kept power from being concentrated in the hands of governmental officials. Each of these checks was motivated by a healthy fear of human nature. The founders believed in human responsibility and human dignity, but they did not trust human nature too much. Their solution was to separate powers and invest each branch with rival powers.

Limited Government

The writers of *The Federalist Papers* realized the futility of trying to remove passions and ambition from the population. They instead divided power and allowed "ambition to counteract ambition." By separating various institutional power structures, they limited the expansion of power.

This included not only a horizontal distribution of powers (separation of powers), but also a vertical distribution of powers (federalism). The federal government was delegated certain powers while the rest of the powers were reserved to the states and the people.

James Madison rightly called this new government a republic which he defined as "a government which derives all its powers directly or indirectly from the great body of people, and is administered by persons holding

---

[43] Madison, *The Federalist Papers*, #51, 322.

their offices during pleasure for a limited period, or during good behavior."[44]

He also argued that "the proposed government cannot be deemed a national one; since its jurisdiction extends to certain enumerated objects only, and leaves to the several states a residuary and inviolable sovereignty over all other objects."[45]

Governmental power was limited by the Constitution and its interpretation was delegated to the judicial branch. As Alexander Hamilton explained, the Constitution was to be the supreme law of the land.

A constitution is, in fact, and must be regarded by the judges as, a fundamental law. It, therefore, belongs to them to ascertain its meaning as well as the meaning of any particular act proceeding from the legislative body. If there should happen to be an irreconcilable variance between the two, that which has the superior obligation and validity ought, of course, to be preferred; or, in other words, the Constitution ought to be preferred to the statute, the intention of the people to the intention of their agents.[46]

Although Hamilton referred to the judiciary as the weakest of the three branches of government, some of the critics of the Constitution warned that the Supreme Court "would be exalted above all power in the government, and subject to no control."[47] Unfortunately, that assessment certain has proved correct over the last few decades.

---

[44] Madison, *The Federalist Papers*, #39, 241.

[45] Ibid., 245.

[46] Alexander Hamilton, *The Federalist Papers*, #78, 467.

[47] Herbert Storing and Murray Day, eds. *The Complete Anti-Federalist* (University of Chicago Press, 1981) II, 420.

The Federalist Papers provide an overview of the political theory that undergirds the U.S. Constitution and provides important insight into the intentions of the framers in constructing a new government. As we have also seen, it shows us where the current governmental structure strays from the original intent of the framers.

The framers fashioned a government that was based upon a realistic view of human nature. The success of this government in large part is due to separating power structures because of their desire to limit the impact of human sinfulness.

CHAPTER 6 The Roots of Freedom

What is freedom? What are the roots of freedom? Answering these questions is not as easy as it may seem. They require some thought and reflection, which for most of us, is a precious commodity.

Fortunately, some of the hard work has been done for us by professor John Danford in his book *Roots of Freedom: A Primer on Modern Liberty*. The material in this book was originally material that was broadcast on Radio Free Europe and Radio Liberty in the late 1980s. Only later did some suggest that the material should be published so that citizens in a free society could also benefit by his work in describing the roots of freedom.

So how does John Danford describe a free society?

> People would surely differ, but what is meant here is a society in which human beings are not "born into" a place—a caste or an occupation, for example—but are free to own property, to raise children, to earn a living, to think, to worship, to express political views, and even to emigrate if desired, and to do so without seeking permission from a master.[48]

Obviously, we all have some constraints on us, but human freedom in a free society would certainly involve the freedom to be able to do the things mentioned above.

Once we define a free society, we can easily see something very disturbing. "Free societies have been rare in human history. They also seem to be fragile—more

---

[48] John W. Danford, *Roots of Freedom: A Primer on Modern Liberty* (Wilmington, DE: ISI Books, 2000), xiv.

fragile than were the dynasties or empires of the ancient world."[49]

In the past, freedom was rare often because of economic necessity. There is little or no freedom for a person who must work every waking hour just to survive. In the ancient world, a free man was free because another was enslaved. A free man was free because he did not need to work for a living.

By the end of the eighteenth century, economic necessity ceased to be the main obstacle to freedom in many places. Yet there were still very few free societies because political power was often concentrated in the hands of a king or dictator (or perhaps in the hands of a few in the ruling class).

Today we have few kings, but we still have many dictators. Free societies also still somewhat rare today. Consider that there are nearly 200 countries in the United Nations, and yet it is probably fair to say that fewer than 50 could truly be called free societies (with functioning democracies).

If nothing else, this study of the roots of freedom should make us thankful, we live in a free country. Free societies are rare in history, and they are still somewhat rare today. We should never take for granted the political and economic freedom we enjoy.

Christian Roots

Danford discusses the roots of liberty in his chapter on "Premodern Christianity." Although we take many of these assumptions (borrowed from Christianity) as basic and obvious, they are important contributions that

---

[49] Ibid., xiv-xv.

provide the foundation for the political freedom we enjoy today.

The first contribution of Christianity was its teaching about the value of the individual. In the Greek and Roman empires, the individual counted for little. "A particular individual was of no consequence when measured against the glory and stability of the empire."[50]

Jesus and his followers taught men and women to think of themselves as significant in the eyes of God. This foundational principle of the dignity and sanctity of human beings was in stark contrast to the prevailing ideas of the day.

Another aspect of this principle was the belief that God was not just the god of a city, or a tribe, or even a nation. The God of the Bible is God over all human beings and savior of all individuals. The belief in the universality of God along with the emphasis on the individual provided an important foundation for liberty because it was "incompatible with the ancient tendency to subordinate the individual entirely to the state or empire."[51]

A second contribution of Christianity involves the linear idea of history. Ancient writers "understood the passage of time in terms of the seasonal rhythms of the natural world."[52] Christianity brought a different perspective by teaching that history is linear. The story of the Bible is the story, after all, of the beginning of the world, human sinfulness, Christ coming to the world, and the eventual culmination of history.

The concept of linear history leads to the idea that circumstances can change over time. If the change is

---

[50] Ibid., 13.

[51] Ibid., 14.

[52] Ibid.

progressive, then over the course of human history there can be progress. "The notion of progress is itself a modern idea, but its roots can be discerned in the Christian doctrine that God enters historical time to save mankind."[53]

A third contribution of Christianity is the principle of the separation of faith from the political realm. Today this is referred to as the separation of church and state. Such an idea was unthinkable in the ancient world. In those cultures, kings and priests were closely connected.

When Jesus was asked by the Pharisees if it was lawful to pay the poll tax (Matt. 22:15-21), He responded by telling them "render to Caesar the things that are Caesar's, and to God the things that are God's." Although it would be many centuries before the full implications of this doctrine were clear, the seeds of spiritual freedom can be found in this Christian teaching.

The fourth contribution of Christianity is the belief in objective truth. While it is true that other philosophers spoke of truth, a Christian perspective on truth is nevertheless an important, additional contribution.

For example, if there is no truth, then "there is no such thing as a just or proper foundation for political rule: whoever gets the power is by definition able to determine what is just or unjust, right or wrong."[54]

In our postmodern world that rejects the idea of objective or absolute truth, all history is merely the history of class struggle. "There is no escape from the endless quest for power, and no space, protected by

---

[53] Ibid., 15-16.

[54] Ibid, 18.

walls of justice, where genuine freedom can be experienced."[55]

This nation was founded on the principle (as articulated in the Declaration of Independence) that there are self-evident truths. As Jesus taught his disciples, "you shall know the truth and the truth shall make you free" (John 8:32).

Thomas Hobbes

Thomas Hobbes was born in England in 1588 and was educated at Oxford in the early 1600s. He was influenced by such men as Francis Bacon (serving as Bacon's secretary for a time) as well as events of the sixteenth and seventeenth centuries. A principal influence was the religious war and conflict of the time (e.g., the Thirty Years War, conflicts in England between Anglicans and Puritans). "Hobbes's two great preoccupations [were]: peace as a goal of the civil order, and a new political science as the means to that goal."[56]

He developed five key principles in his political science. The first is that individuals are more fundamental than any social order. To understand humans, he would argue, we must go back to a "state of nature" which would represent the condition human beings would be in if all the conventions and laws of political society were removed.

Hobbes also argued that humans are equal politically. "No one can be viewed as politically superior, because every human being is vulnerable to violent death at the hands of his fellows."[57] The natural condition of

---

[55] Ibid., 20.

[56] Ibid., 77.

[57] Ibid., 83.

mankind, he says, is "solitary, poor, nasty, brutish, and short."[58]

Hobbes, therefore, argues in his second principle that the natural need for self-preservation is the only true reason people live in political communities. In other words, we live in political communities to satisfy individual needs of human nature such as life and security.

Third, Hobbes argues that because these needs are universal (and scientifically demonstrable), they provide a basis for agreement and a peaceful political order. He argues that we should "be willing, when others are so too, as far-forth as for peace, and defense of himself he shall think it necessary, to lay down this right to all things, and be contented with so much liberty against other men, as he would allow other men against himself."[59]

Fourth, since political society exists for self-preservation, no one can ever give up the right to self-defense. A cardinal principle of a liberal society is that no man can be compelled to confess a crime or to testify against himself in court.

Finally, all legitimate government rests on a contract consented to (at least tacitly) by individuals. Hobbes calls this agreement a "covenant" because it is an open-ended contract, a promise that must be continually fulfilled in the future.

Hobbes also argued that a sovereign must enforce this covenant because "covenants without the sword are but words."[60] But though he justified a powerful

---

[58] Thomas Hobbes, *Leviathan* (Indianapolis: Hackett Publishing, 1994), 76.

[59] Ibid., 80.

[60] Ibid., 106.

government or sovereign, it was a perspective that was challenged by others like John Locke who believed that even the sovereign must be limited.

John Locke

John Locke was the son of a Puritan who fought with Oliver Cromwell. Though he was not an orthodox Puritan like his father, he was nevertheless a sincere Christian, who believed that the Bible was "infallibly true."

Locke argued in his *Two Treatises of Government* that men form societies "for the mutual preservation of their lives, liberties, and estates, which I call by the general name, property."[61] On the one hand, he wrote that material things are not owned by anyone but exist in common for all men. "God, as King David says, (Psalm 115:16) has given the earth to the children of men, given it to mankind in common."[62] But on the other hand, he also acknowledged that we do take possession of things and thus make them our property.

> He that is nourished by the acorns he picked under an oak, or the apples he gathered from the trees in the wood, has certainly appropriated them to himself. Nobody can deny but the nourishment is his. I ask then, When did they begin to be his? When he digested? Or when he ate? Or when he boiled? Or when he brought them home? Or when he picked them up? And 'tis plain, if the first gathering made them not his, nothing else

---

[61] John Locke, *Two Treatises of Government*, ed. Peter Laslett (Cambridge: Cambridge University Press, 1960), Second Treatise, Par. 123, 395.

[62] Ibid., Par. 25, 327.

could. That labor put a distinction between them and common. That added something to them more than nature, the common mother of all, had done; and so they became his private property.[63]

Locke also argued that land is ultimately worthless until labor it added to it. He even goes on to argue that wealth is almost wholly the product of human labor (he says 999/1000 of the value of things is the result of labor).

He also argued that "Men being, as has been said, by nature, all free, equal and independent, no one can be put out of this estate, and subjected to the political power of another, without his own consent."[64] He acknowledged that each man or woman is born free and becomes a member of a commonwealth by agreeing to accept its protections, but most commonly this is done by what Locke call "tacit consent."

Finally, Locke also focused his concern about the possibility of an oppressive government, so he insisted on the necessity of limiting the sovereign power as much as possible. The legislature cannot "take from any man any part of his property without his own consent."[65]

Locke also insisted on one final limitation of the power of government: the citizenry. He writes, "yet the legislative being only a fiduciary power to act for certain ends, there remains still in the people of supreme power to remove or alter the legislative, when they find the legislative to act contrary to the trust reposed in them."[66]

---

[63] Ibid., Par 28, 329-330.

[64] Ibid., Par. 95, 375.

[65] Ibid., Par. 138, 406.

[66] Ibid., Par. 149, 413.

American Liberty

The ideas of freedom found their way to the American shore as disruptions of the English civil war drove many English subjects to the New World. In their travels, "they took with them as much of the system of English liberty as would survive the Atlantic crossing."[67]

Some of the settlers established civil compacts (or what Locke would later call social contracts). Perhaps the best known is the Mayflower Compact, which was a political covenant binding the pilgrims together into "a civil body politic." Most of these American settlements involved self-government simply because the powers that originally granted them their charters were thousands of miles away.

America's founding document is the Declaration of Independence. The ideas of John Locke can certainly be found within this document. The Declaration states the principle from Locke that "all men are created equal." It also follows his thinking by stating, "That to secure these rights, governments are instituted among men, deriving their just powers from the consent of the governed."

All the writers during the founding period (Thomas Jefferson, James Madison, George Washington, John Adams, Benjamin Franklin, Alexander Hamilton) were "deeply learned in English history, political history generally, and the history of political thought back to Aristotle and Plato. References to Cicero, Tacitus, and Plutarch dot their pages, along with frequent allusions to republics as diverse as Venice, Holland, Geneva, Sparta, and Rome."[68]

Alexander Hamilton, writing in *The Federalist Papers*, said that the American people would decide

---

[67] Danford, 146.

[68] Ibid., 149.

"whether societies of men are really capable or not of establishing good government from reflection and choice, or whether they are forever destined to depend for their political constitutions on accident and force."[69]

James Madison, in *The Federalist Papers*, addressed two key issues in American government: factions and limiting governmental power. He suggested that the large federal republic made it more difficult for factions to gain power and oppress others.

Limiting the power of government was accomplished by separating power. "Ambition must counteract ambition. The interest of the man must be connected with the constitutional rights of the place."[70] The framers pursued "the policy of supplying, by opposite and rival interests" to these various branches of government.

As an extra precaution, the framers also divided the legislature (because it was expected to be the most powerful and dangerous branch) into two different houses. They also decided to "render them, by different modes of election and different principles of action, as little connected with each other as the nature of their common functions and their common dependence on the society will admit."[71]

They further protected individual rights by adding the Bill of Rights. These amendments explicitly deny power to the government to interfere with specific individual freedoms. The rights and freedoms we enjoy today developed over time through Christian influence and key writers in the Western tradition.

---

[69] Alexander Hamilton, *The Federalist Papers* (New York: New American Library, 1961), No. 1, 33.

[70] Ibid., No. 51, 322.

[71] Ibid.

SECTION 3 Church and State Issues

CHAPTER 7 Separation of Church and State

Wall of Separation

When Thomas Jefferson first used the phrase "wall of separation," it is certain that he would never have anticipated the controversy that surrounds that term two centuries later. The metaphor has become so powerful that more Americans are more familiar with Jefferson's phrase than with the actual language of the Constitution.[72]

In one sense, the idea of separation of church and state is an accurate description of what must take place between the two institutions. History is full of examples (e.g., the Inquisition) of the dangers that arise when the institutions of church and state become too intertwined.

But the contemporary concept of separation of church and state goes far beyond the recognition that the two institutions must be separate. The current version of this phrase has come to mean that there should be a complete separation between religion and public life.

At the outset, we should state the obvious: the phrase "separation of church and state" is not in the Constitution. Although that should be an obvious statement, it is amazing how many citizens (including lawyers and politicians) do not know that simple fact.

Since the phrase is not in the Constitution and not even significantly discussed by the framers (e.g., *The Federalist Papers*), it is open to wide interpretation and misinterpretation. The only clear statement about religion

---

[72] Barbara Perry, "Justice Hugo Black and the Wall of Separation between Church and State," *Journal of Church and State* 31 (1989): 55.

in the Constitution can be found in the First Amendment, and we will look at its legislative history later in this article.

Thomas Jefferson used the phrase "separation of church and state" when he wrote to the Danbury Baptist Association in 1802. Then the phrase slipped into obscurity. In 1947, Justice Hugo Black revived it in the case of *Everson v. Board of Education*. He wrote that the First Amendment "was intended to erect a wall of separation between church and State." He added that this wall "must be kept high and impregnable."[73]

The wall metaphor revived by Justice Black has been misused ever since. For example, the wall of separation has been used to argue that nearly any religious activity (prayer, Bible reading, moment of silence) and any religious symbol (cross, creche, Ten Commandments, etc.) is impermissible outside of church and home. Most of these activities and symbols have been stripped from public arenas. As we will see, it doesn't appear that Jefferson intended anything of the sort with his metaphor.

It's also worth noting that six of the thirteen original states had official, state-sponsored churches. Some states (Connecticut, Georgia, Maryland, Massachusetts, New Hampshire, and South Carolina) even refused to ratify the new Constitution unless it included a prohibition of federal involvement in the state churches.

History of the Phrase

So what was the meaning of "separation of church and state" and how has it changed? Some history is in order.

---

[73] *Everson v. Board of Education*, 330 U.S., 16, 18.

The presidential campaign of 1800 was one of the most bitterly contested presidential elections in American history. Republican Thomas Jefferson defeated Federalist John Adams (who served as Vice-President under George Washington). During the campaign, the Federalists attacked Jefferson's religious beliefs, arguing that he was an "atheist" and an "infidel." Some were so fearful of a Jefferson presidency, they buried their family Bibles or hid them in wells fearing that President Jefferson would confiscate them.[74] Timothy Dwight (President of Yale College) even warned a few years before that if Jefferson *were* elected, "we may see the Bible cast into a bonfire."[75] These concerns were unwarranted since Jefferson had written a great deal in the previous two decades about his support of religious liberty.

In the midst of these concerns, the loyal Republicans of the Danbury Baptist Association wrote to the president congratulating him on his election and his dedication to religious liberty. President Jefferson used the letter as an opportunity to explain why he did not declare days of public prayer and thanksgiving as Washington and Adams had done so before him.

In his letter to them on New Year's Day 1802, Jefferson agreed with their desire for religious freedom saying that religious faith was a matter between God and man. Jefferson also affirmed his belief in the First Amendment and went on to say that he believed it denied Congress (or the President) the right to dictate religious beliefs. He argued that the First Amendment denied the Federal government this power:

---

[74] Dumas Malone, *Jefferson and His Time*, vol. 3, *Jefferson and the Ordeal of Liberty* (Boston: Little, Brown, 1962), 481.

[75] Timothy Dwight, *The Duty of Americans, at the Present Crisis*, reprinted in Ellis Sandoz, ed., *Political Sermons of the American Founding Era, 1730-1805* (Indianapolis, IN: Liberty Press, 1991), 1382.

Believing with you that religion is a matter which lies solely between man and his God, that he owes account to none other for his faith or his worship, that the legislative powers of government reach actions only, and not opinion, I contemplate with sovereign reverence that act of the whole American people which declared that their legislature should "make no law respecting an establishment of religion, or prohibiting the free exercise thereof," thus building a wall of separation between Church and State.[76]

It appears that Jefferson's phrase actually came from the 1800 election. Federalist ministers spoke against Jefferson "often from their pulpits, excoriating his infidelity and deism."[77] Republicans, therefore, argued that clergymen should not preach about politics but maintain a separation between the two.

We might add that a century and a half before Jefferson wrote to the Danbury Baptists, Roger Williams erected a "hedge or wall of separation" in a tract he wrote in 1644. Williams used the metaphor to illustrate the need to protect the church from the world. Otherwise, the garden of the church would turn into a wilderness.[78] While it might be possible that Jefferson borrowed the metaphor from Roger Williams, it appears

---

[76] Thomas Jefferson's letter to the Danbury Baptist Association, January 1, 1802, www.loc.gov/loc/lcib/9806/danpre.html.

[77] Philip Hamburger, *Separation of Church and State* (Cambridge, MA: Harvard University Press, 2002) 111.

[78] Roger Williams, "Mr. Cotton's Letter Lately Printed, Examined and Answered," in *The Complete Writings of Roger Williams* (Providence, RI: Providence Press, 1866), 1:392.

that Jefferson was not familiar with Williams' use of the metaphor.[79]

Jefferson used his letter to the Danbury Baptists to make a key point about his executive power. In the letter, he argued that the president had no authority to proclaim a religious holiday. He believed that governmental authority belonged only to individual states. Essentially, Jefferson's wall of separation applied only to the national government.

Although the Danbury letter was published in newspapers, the "wall of separation" metaphor never gained much attention and essentially slipped into obscurity. In 1879 the metaphor entered the lexicon of American constitutional law in the case of *Reynolds v. United States*. The court stated that Jefferson's Danbury letter "may be accepted almost as an authoritative declaration of the scope and effects of the [First] Amendment thus secured."[80] Although it was mentioned in this opinion, there is good evidence to believe that Jefferson's metaphor "played no role" in the Supreme Court's decision.[81]

In 1947, Justice Hugo L. Black revived Jefferson's wall metaphor in the case of *Everson v. Board of Education*. He applied this phrase in a different way from Thomas Jefferson. Black said that the First Amendment "was intended to erect a wall of separation between

---

[79] Edwin Gaustad, *Sworn on the Altar of God: A Religious Biography of Thomas Jefferson* (Grand Rapids, Mich.: William B Eerdmans, 1996), 72.

[80] *Reynolds v. United States*, 98 U.S. 145, 164.

[81] Robert M. Hutchins, "The Future of the Wall," in *The Wall between Church and State*, ed. Dallin H. Oaks (Chicago: University of Chicago Press, 1963), 17.

church and State." He added that this wall "must be kept high and impregnable."[82]

Daniel Dreisbach, the author of *Thomas Jefferson and the Wall of Separation Between Church and State*, shows that Black's wall differs from Jefferson's wall. "Although Justice Black credited the third president with building the 'wall of separation,' the barrier raised in *Everson* differs from Jefferson's in function and location."[83]

The wall erected by Justice Black is "high and impregnable." On the other hand, Jefferson "occasionally lowered the 'wall' if there were extenuating circumstances. For example, he approved treaties with Indian tribes which underwrote the 'propagation of the Gospel among the Heathen.'"[84]

There is also a difference in the location of the two walls. Whereas Jefferson's "wall" explicitly separated the institutions of church and state, Black's wall, more expansively, separates religion and all civil government. Moreover, Jefferson's "wall" separated church and the federal government only. By incorporating the First Amendment nonestablishment provision into the due process clause of the Fourteenth Amendment, Black's wall separates religion and civil government at all levels—federal, state, and local.[85]

Jefferson's metaphor was a statement about federalism (the relationship between the federal

---

[82] *Everson v. Board of Education*, 330 U.S., 16, 18.

[83] Daniel Dreisbach, *Thomas Jefferson and the Wall of Separation Between Church and State* (New York: New York University Press, 2002), 125.

[84] Derek H. Davis, "Wall of Separation Metaphor," *Journal of Church and State*, vol. 45(1), Winter 2003.

[85] Dreisbach, *Thomas Jefferson*, 125.

government and the states). But Black turned it into a wall between religion and government (which because of the incorporation of the Fourteenth Amendment could also be applied to state and local governments).

First Amendment

How did we get the wording of the First Amendment? Once we understand its legislative history, we can understand the perspective of those who drafted the Bill of Rights.[86]

James Madison (architect of the Constitution) is the one who first proposed the wording of what became the First Amendment. On June 8, 1789 Madison proposed the following:

"The civil rights of none shall be abridged on account of religious belief or worship, nor shall any national religion be established, nor shall the full and equal rights of conscience be in any manner, or on any pretext, infringed."

The representatives debated this wording and then turned the task over to a committee consisting of Madison and ten other House members. They proposed a new version that read:

"No religion shall be established by law, nor shall the equal rights of conscience be infringed."

This wording was debated. During the debate, Madison explained, "he apprehended the meaning of the words to be, that Congress should not establish a religion, and enforce the legal observation of it by law,

---

[86] The details of the debate on the First Amendment can be found in the Annals of Congress. *The Debates and Proceedings in the Congress of the United States.* "History of Congress." 42 vols. Washington, D.C.: Gales & Seaton, 1834-1856.

nor compel men to worship God in any manner contrary to their conscience."

Representative Benjamin Huntington complained that the proposed wording might "be taken in such latitude as to be extremely hurtful to the cause of religion." So Madison suggested inserting the word "national" before the word "religion." He believed that this would reduce the fears of those concerned over the establishment of a national religion. After all, some were concerned America might drift in the direction of Europe where countries have a state-sponsored religion that citizens were often compelled to accept and even fund.

Representative Gerry balked at the word "national," because he argued, the Constitution created a federal government, not a national one. So Madison withdrew his latest proposal but assured Congress his reference to a "national religion" had to do with a national religious establishment, not a national government.

A week later, the House again altered the wording to this:

"Congress shall make no law establishing religion, or to prevent the free exercise thereof, or to infringe the rights of conscience."

Meanwhile, the Senate debated other versions of the same amendment and on Sept. 3, 1789, came up with this wording:

"Congress shall make no law establishing articles of faith or a mode of worship, or prohibiting the free exercise of religion."

The House didn't like the Senate's changes and called for a conference, from which emerged the wording ultimately included in the Bill of Rights:

"Congress shall make no law respecting an establishment of religion, or prohibiting the free exercise thereof."

As we can see, Congress was attempting to prevent the establishment of a national religion or a national church with their drafting of the First Amendment.

Separation, Sponsorship, and Accommodation

How should the government relate to the church? Should there be a separation of church and state? Essentially there are three answers to these questions: separation, sponsorship, and accommodation.

At one end of the spectrum of opinion is strict separation of church and state. Proponents of this position advocate the complete separation of any religious activity (prayer, Bible reading) and any religious symbol (cross, Ten Commandments) from government settings. Richard John Neuhaus called this "the naked public square" because religious values are stripped from the public arena.[87]

Proponents of this view would oppose any direct or indirect benefit to religion or religious organizations from the government. This would include opposition to tuition tax credits, education vouchers, and government funding of faith-based organizations.

At the other end of the spectrum would be sponsorship of religious organizations.

Proponents would support school prayer, Bible reading in public schools and the posting of the Ten Commandments in classrooms and public places.

---

[87] Richard John Neuhaus, *The Naked Public Square: Religion and Democracy in America* (William B. Eerdmans Publishing Co., 1984).

Proponents would also support tuition tax credits, education vouchers, and funding of faith-based organizations.

Between these two views is accommodation. Proponents argue that government should not sponsor religion but neither should it be hostile to religion. Government can accommodate religious activities. Government should provide protection for the church and provide for the free expression of religion. But government should not favor a particular group or religion over another.

Proponents would oppose direct governmental support of religious schools but would support education vouchers since the parents would be free to use the voucher at a public, private school, or Christian school. Proponents would oppose mandated school prayer but support programs that provide equal access to students. Equal access argues that if students are allowed to start a debate club or chess club on campus, they should also be allowed to start a Bible club.

We should reject the idea of a "naked public square" (where religious values have been stripped from the public arena). And we should also reject the idea of a "sacred public square" (where religious ideas are sponsored by government). We should seek an "open public square" (where government neither censors nor sponsors religion but accommodates religion).

Government should not be hostile toward religion, but neither should it sponsor religion or favor a particular faith over another. Government should maintain a benevolent neutrality toward religion and accommodate religious activities and symbols.

CHAPTER 8 Different Views About Church and State

As we explained in the previous chapter, the idea of a "high wall of separation" first entered into our nation's judicial conscience in the 1947 *Everson v. Board of Education* case. Although the court decided to allow public funding for the transportation of Catholic school students, it invoked the "high wall" doctrine as a rule for determining the future use of public funds. Justice Hugo Black appealed to Supreme Court precedent as well as the intent of the Founding Fathers in winning his 5-4 decision which included the "high wall" language. Justice Black wrote that our founders "reached the conviction that individual religious liberty could be achieved best under a government which was stripped of all power to tax, to support, or otherwise to assist any or all religions, or to interfere with the beliefs of any religious individual or group."[88] This 1947 decision became the catalyst for a growing debate in the last half of the 20th century regarding the relationship between faith and government in America.

The phrase *high wall of separation* has divided Americans into a number of different groups depending upon their theological and political leanings. Some feel that the high court drastically overstepped the original meaning of Jefferson's words, going far beyond his original intent. Others applaud the Court's attempt to separate once and for all this country's bias towards Christianity, especially its Protestant wing. Since the question often revolves around the original intent of the Founding Fathers, many seek to determine whether or

---

[88] Wayne House, ed., *Restoring The Constitution* (Dallas, TX: Probe Books, 1987), 298.

not the Founders supported a Christian state, a secular state, or something in between.

All of this points to a few important questions faced by Christians. How should individual believers and the church as a whole relate to the state and its various institutions? What about the role individuals should take in politics, efforts to reform government, and attempts to pass laws that make our society behave more "biblically"? In this article we will look at three different responses to these questions and examine some of the pros and cons of each. Since every believer is limited in both their time and resources, it is important to think carefully about where we focus our efforts in furthering God's kingdom. The purpose of this discussion is not to question anyone's commitment to Christ, but to merely step back and look at some of the underlying assumptions held by each of these three positions.

Anti-Religious Separatists

Americans support the notion of separation of church and state by a small majority.[89] Just what we mean by *separate* seems to be the real issue. Some go as far as to argue that any position on public policy that is motivated by a religious belief is out of bounds and should not receive a hearing. This group, who might be called "anti-religious separatists," argues that religion is fine as long as it does not invade the public sphere. Religion must impact only private morality; if it leaks into the public square where policy making actually occurs, it is inappropriate at best. There are many examples of such anti-religious bias. Writing about a speech that Ronald Reagan made that included religious overtones, a *New York Times* article said, "You don't have to be a secular

---

[89] Stephen V. Monsma, *Positive Neutrality* (Grand Rapids, MI: Baker Books, 1993), 57.

humanist to take offense at that display of what, in America, should be private piety. . . . Americans ask piety in Presidents, not displays of religious preference. Mr. Reagan uttered not just an ecumenical summons to the spirit. He was pandering to the Christian right that helped to propel his national political career."[90] Another presidential candidate wrote, "No president should attempt to transform policy debates into theological disputes."[91] Some believe the separation of church and state to mean a complete separation of religious values from public policy debates.

It's one thing to complain of inappropriate public piety, it is quite another to apply an anti-religious bias to court decisions and other actions that affect all Americans, religious or not. In one of the most important Supreme Court decisions on the separation of church and state in regards to education, Justices William Douglas and Hugo Black concurred that religious schools are by nature harmful. Writing specifically about Catholics schools they said:

> The whole education of the child is filled with propaganda. That, of course, is the very purpose of such schools, the very reason for going to all of the work and expense of maintaining a dual school system. Their purpose is not so much to educate, but to indoctrinate and train, not to teach Scripture truths and Americanism, but to make loyal Roman Catholics. The children are regimented, and are told what to wear, what to do, and what to think.[92]

---

[90] Ibid., 63.

[91] Ibid.

[92] Ibid., 71.

Although this quote refers specifically to Catholic schools, its description could apply to many types of private religious schools. This caricature of private Christian schools, that they do not teach but indoctrinate, that they fail to convey Americanism (whatever that is), is still a concern of many who have observed and objected to the recent rapid growth in private schooling.

Those who hold an "anti-religious separatist" viewpoint often talk positively of an American civil religion. The idea is that some religion might be better than no religion at all, but it must never actually enter into policy decisions. A thin veneer of religion is all that is needed. An example might be President Dwight Eisenhower urging Americans to spend the first Fourth of July holiday of his administration in prayer and penance. He then proceeded to fish in the morning, go golfing in the afternoon, and play cards all evening.[93]

When Christians advocate such a vague form of public religion, they do great harm to the faith. A lukewarm civil religion does not address the redeeming sacrifice that makes Christianity what it is. Nor does it value the revealed knowledge found in the Bible. The idea of providing America with a nonpreferential treatment of religion is legitimate. The danger lies in the promotion or religious activity that waters down the beliefs of the various faiths, both Christian and non-Christian.

Christian America

It is a popular notion among Christians that America was founded as a Christian nation, and that the goal of believers everywhere should be to place our government back into the hands of committed Christians who hold

---

[93] George Will, "Who Put Morality In Politics?" *Newsweek*, 1980.

acceptable views on theological and moral issues. As a corollary to this position, it follows that our nation's institutions, its schools, courts, regulatory commissions, etc, should be established on Christian principles.

Various Christian groups use language that supports this view. The Christian Coalition, Eagle Forum, Concerned Women for America, and others often present this perspective. Jerry Falwell stated, "Any diligent student of American history finds that our great nation was founded by godly men upon godly principles to be a Christian nation."[94] John Whitehead, in his 1977 book *The Separation Illusion*, wrote, "In recent years Christians and non-Christians alike have been questioning whether America was ever a Christian nation. Without doubt, it was, but secular historians have eradicated as much Christian influence as possible from history."[95]

Pat Robertson began the Christian Coalition in response to this perceived conspiracy to purge our history and government from Christianity. Stating its goals, its executive director said, "What Christians have got to do is take back this country, one precinct at a time, one neighborhood at a time, and one state at a time. I honestly believe that in my lifetime we will see a country once again governed by Christians . . . and Christian values."[96]

Those who hold to this view are generally comfortable with making Christianity the semi-established religion of America. Everywhere the government is involved in our lives would take on a Christian flavor. Every citizen, regardless of religious affiliation, would be

---

[94] Monsma, *Neutrality*, 73.

[95] John Whitehead, *The Separation Illusion* (Milford, MI: Mott Media, 1977), 17.

[96] Monsma, *Neutrality*, 73.

responsible for understanding and adjusting to this ubiquitous Christian culture.

To many, this would be doing to those of other faiths, including atheists, just what we have been accusing them of doing to Christians. Forcing people to separate their public lives from their beliefs and thus denying them their first amendment freedom of religion.

There is no question that we have been blessed as a nation because our Founding Fathers built our government on Christian principles regarding human nature and a theistic view of reality. We enjoy common grace as a people when our laws conform to God's standard of justice. The question that we must ask is, Can we as Christians can impose a biblical culture on a majority who no longer acknowledge the authority of Scripture? Since only 32 percent of Americans agree that: "The government should take special steps to protect the Judeo-Christian heritage," this question is more than theoretical.[97] Perhaps a better goal would be to work for a government based on the concepts of freedom and neutrality with regards to religion.

Positive Neutrality

The idea of positive neutrality begins with the assumption that both religious structures and the state possess a certain degree of sovereignty over their respective domains. Each possess certain rights and responsibilities and should be free to operate without interference from the other. As the Dutch Protestant Abraham Kuyper stated it: "The sovereignty of the State and the sovereignty of the Church exist side by side, and they mutually limit each other."[98] Christians can find

[97] Ibid., 57.

[98] Ibid., 179.

support for this view in biblical passages that describe both the church and the state as divinely ordained realities (1 Peter 2 and Romans 13).

Positive neutrality argues that religious organizations have both rights and responsibilities. According to Stephen Monsma, author of *Positive Neutrality*, religious groups have the right to develop and teach their core beliefs, to shape their member's behavior and attitudes, to provide a wide range of services to members and non-members, and to participate in the policy-making process of our republic. On the responsibility side, religious organizations must both accept and seek to enhance the authority and legitimacy of the state and encourage its members to obey its lawful decisions. Religious groups should also seek to develop civic virtue that enhances public life and not attempt to take over those things given to the state to perform. This does not mean that religious groups do not have the right to criticize the state; it means that they may not work to remove its legitimacy.

According to the notion of positive neutrality, the state also has certain rights and responsibilities. The government should make decisions that coordinate, protect, encourage, and empower society's various spheres of influence (including the religious sphere) with the goal of promoting justice, the public interest, the common good, or some other similar goal. The state is not to transgress the sovereignty of the other spheres although there are times when it is appropriate for the state to give material aid, in a neutral manner, to organizations in another sphere.

The immediate impact of moving towards a system of positive neutrality would be reflected in three areas. First, our political system would have to tolerate and accommodate a wider range of religious practices. Second, the state would have to protect the right of religious groups to influence public policies. And finally, rather than working only through secularly based groups and programs, the government would fund the activities of both religious and secular groups for the purpose of providing needed social programs. These changes may be possible only by dropping the "secular purpose" part of what is known as the Lemon test, a three-part test for appropriate government spending resulting from the *Lemon v. Kurtzman* Supreme Court case in 1971.

What this means, in effect, is that when the government gives financial aid to schools, homeless shelters, day care, or other agencies, it cannot discriminate against religiously based organizations. To continue to do so shows a bias towards secular organizations, motivations, and ideals.

Religion in School

We have considered three views of how the church and the state should relate to each other. The first was the anti-religious separatists. This group included those who desire what could be called a naked public square, naked of any religious influence. The second was the Christian America perspective; it advocates a sacred public square and the semi-establishment of the Christian religion. The third view is called positive neutrality, which argues for an open public square. The first two positions discriminate against the religious rights of Christians or non-Christians; the last treats all religious groups equally and does not favor secular organizations over religious ones.

Let us look at the specific issue of religion in our schools and see how the notion of positive neutrality might change what we consider to be constitutional and what isn't. Currently, the Court uses a three-part test to determine constitutionality. First, a program must have a secular purpose. Second, it cannot further a religious effect, and finally, it may not cause excessive entanglement between religion and the state. In its attempt at applying these rules, the Court has created a very unclear line of what is permissible and what is not. It has forbidden state-composed prayers, Bible reading, reading of the Lord's Prayer, posting the Ten Commandments, a minute of silence for meditation and prayer, mandating the teaching of evidence for creationism, and certain types of prayers at graduation ceremonies. However, it has permitted release time programs held off campus for religious instruction, teaching about religion, transportation for private school children, a minute of silence for meditation, and voluntary, student-led and -initiated religious clubs.

The obvious result of the Lemon test has been a bias against the religious and for the secular, not neutrality. In trying to account for local religious practices, some justices have argued that prayer and religious celebrations are actually secular and traditional activities rather than acts of worship. This tactic satisfies no one. Positive neutrality argues for a full and free play of all religious groups and of both religion and secularism. True neutrality is achieved by welcoming and encouraging all religions and secular philosophies to participate in the open marketplace of ideas on campus.

True neutrality could be accomplished in our public schools by applying the equal access principle the Court used in *Westside Community Schools v. Mergen.* This decision treated all extracurricular clubs, both religious and secular, with neutrality. This principle could be applied to prayer, the study of origins, and the posting of the Ten Commandments. In effect, this would remove some of the anti-religious bias that pervades public schools.

Neutrality is also enhanced when the government encourages educational choice by funding private schools regardless of their religious or non-religious nature. By allowing vouchers for parents to use to send their children to religious schools of their choice, the government would be treating religious and non-religious schools in a neutral manner.

Positive neutrality insists that religious ideas should never be forced to hide themselves behind secular ones in order to participate in the public square. The government is not being neutral when it endorses a secular idea over a religious one in our schools or in other social programs. While many Americans are unhappy with the government's current bias against religious beliefs, it remains to be seen if they are ready for real religious freedom that would allow full participation in the public realm by all faiths and philosophies.

SECTION 4 Political Discourse

CHAPTER 9 Politics and Religion

Legislating Morality

Nearly everywhere you go, it seems, you hear statements like, "You can't legislate morality," or "Christians shouldn't try to legislate their morality." Like dandelions, they pop up out of nowhere and sow seeds of deception in the fertile, secular soil of our society.

Unfortunately, I have also heard these clichés repeated in many churches. Even Christians seem confused about how they are to communicate a biblical view of issues to a secular world.

Part of the confusion stems from blurring the distinctions between law and human behavior. When a person says, "You can't legislate morality," he or she might mean simply that you can't make people good through legislation. In that instance, Christians can agree.

The law (whether biblical law or civil law) does not by itself transform human behavior. The apostle Paul makes that clear in his epistle to the Romans. English jurists for the last few centuries have also agreed that the function of the law is not to make humans good but to control criminal behavior.

However, if you understand the question in its normal formulation, then Christians can and should legislate morality. At the more basic level, law and public policy is an attempt to legislate morality. The more relevant question is not whether we should legislate morality but what kind of morality we should legislate.

Much of the confusion stems from our country's misunderstanding of democratic pluralism. Our founders wisely established a country that protected individual personal beliefs with constitutional guarantees of speech, assembly, and religion. However, undergirding this pluralism was a legal foundation that presupposed a Judeo-Christian system of ethics.

Thus, in the area of personal ethics, people are free to think and believe anything they want. Moreover, they are free to practice a high degree of ethical pluralism in their personal life. To use a common phrase, they are free "to do their own thing." However, that doesn't imply total ethical anarchy. Not everyone can "do his own thing" in every arena of life, so government must set some limits to human behavior.

This is the domain of social ethics. To use an oft-repeated phrase, "a person's right to freely swing his or her arms, stops at the end of your nose." When one person's actions begin to affect another person, we have moved from personal ethics to social ethics and often have to place some limits on human behavior.

Government is to bear the sword (Rom. 13:4) and thus must legislate some minimum level of morality when there is a threat to life, liberty, or property. An arsonist is not free "to do his own thing" nor is a rapist or a murderer. At that point, government must step in to protect the rights of citizens.

Perhaps the most visible clash between different perceptions of ethics can be seen in the abortion controversy. Pro-choice groups generally see the abortion issue as an area of personal morality. On the other hand, pro-life advocates respond that the fetus is human life, so something else is involved besides just personal choice. Thus, government should protect the life of the unborn child.

Promoting Christian Values

Christians must consider how to communicate biblical morality effectively to a secular culture. Here are a few principles.

First, we must interpret Scripture properly. Too often, Christians have passed off their sociological preferences (on issues like abortion or homosexual behavior) instead of doing proper biblical exegesis. The result has often been *a priori* conclusions buttressed with improper proof-texting.

In areas where the Bible clearly speaks, we should exercise our prophetic voice as we seek to be salt and light (Matt. 5:13-16). In other areas, concessions should be allowed.

The apostle Paul recognized that the first priority of Christians is to preach the gospel. He refused to allow various distinctions to hamper his effectiveness and tried to "become all things to all men" that he might save some (1 Cor. 9:22). Christians must stand firm for biblical truth, yet also recognize the greater need for the unsaved person to hear a loving presentation of the gospel.

Second, Christians should carefully develop biblical principles that can be applied to contemporary social and medical issues. Christians often jump immediately from biblical passages into political and social programs. They wrongly neglect the important intermediate step of applying biblical principles within a particular social and cultural situation.

In recent years, there has been a dangerous tendency for certain Christians to identify their message with a particular political party or philosophy of government. Christians must be more careful to articulate the connection between biblical principles and specific programs. While Christians may agree about the goal, they may reasonably disagree about which program might best achieve that goal. In these non-moral areas, a spirit of freedom may be necessary.

Third, Christians should articulate the moral teachings of Scripture in ways that are meaningful in a pluralistic society. Philosophical principles like the "right to life" or "the dangers of promiscuity" can be appealed to as part of common grace. Scientific, social, legal, and ethical considerations can be useful in arguing for biblical principles in a secular culture.

Christians can argue in a public arena against abortion on the basis of scientific and legal evidence. Medical advances in embryology and fetology show that human life exists in the womb. A legal analysis of the Supreme Court's *Roe v. Wade* decision shows the justices violated a standard principle of jurisprudence. The burden of proof is placed on the life-taker, and the benefit of the doubt is given to the life-saver. Since the Court never determined when life begins, they erroneously ruled that states could not prohibit first trimester abortions.

Likewise, Christians can argue against the depravity of homosexuality on the basis of the dangers of sexual promiscuity in an age of AIDS. Epidemiological and sociological data can provide a convincing case for public health measures that will prevent the spread of AIDS.

This does not mean we should sublimate the biblical message. But our effectiveness in the public arena will be improved if we elaborate the scientific, social, legal, and ethical aspects of a particular issue instead of trying to articulate our case on Scripture alone.

Christians should develop effective ways to communicate biblical morality to our secular culture. Law and public policy should be based upon biblical morality that results from an accurate interpretation of Scripture and a careful application to society.

Role of Religion in Politics

What should be the role of religion in politics? Many years ago, I participated in a panel representing a Baskin-Robbins variety of religious opinion that considered this controversial question. The scenario we were to consider was that of "a candidate running for office who comes from the far religious right and uses his religious beliefs as a major part of his political credentials."

I was intrigued by the addition of the adjective "far," especially since the moderator, Hodding Carter, served in the administration of an evangelical president. Jimmy Carter–hardly considered a member of the "far" religious right–became the only Democrat to win a presidential election in the last twenty years because he successfully used his "born-again" beliefs to influence voters.

Moreover, how plausible is the scenario? Although the evangelical vote is still significant in certain Republican primaries, it hardly represents a monolithic voting block. In anything, there are many surveys that suggest American voters still have some misgivings about mixing politics and evangelical Christianity.

Over the last three decades, we have seen political candidates running who have ministerial degrees or close ties to churches or seminaries. Some have been successful, while others have not fared that well in their campaign.

On the other side have been warnings from the ACLU, People for the American Way, and Americans United for the Separation of Church and State about the dangers of such Christians who are "religious ayatollahs" and want to "establish a theocracy in America." Most citizens ignore these hyperbolic warnings, but some truly fear anyone in office who is too vocal about his or her Christianity.

Certainly, the evangelical vote has played a factor in past presidential elections. Jimmy Carter won one of the closest elections in American history because of the "born-again" vote and lost it four years later when many of those voters abandoned him for Ronald Reagan.

George W. Bush won the closest election in American history and could attribute much of his victory to the evangelical vote. Bill Clinton and Barack Obama, on the other hand, won without getting a majority of the evangelical vote. Candidates with a pastoral background (like Mike Huckabee) or who made an explicit appeal to evangelicals (like Ted Cruz) haven't faired so well in the primaries. Other candidates who were obviously not evangelicals (Mitt Romney, Donald Trump) won the Republican nomination.

Here is an irony. The Constitution prohibits a religious test for public office, but the voters may be reversing that idea. They seem to want someone of faith but might be fearful of someone who takes his faith too seriously.

Thirty years ago, President Eisenhower declared a national day of prayer and then used the day to go golfing. Later revelations from the Reagan White House suggest the president (or at least Nancy Reagan) spent more time consulting the stars than praying to the Creator of those stars. Perhaps nothing has changed. If so, then the hypothetical scenario we were asked to consider on the panel will remain hypothetical.

Pluralism in this Country

This country was founded on the idea of a tempered pluralism that allowed for a civil debate among the citizens. Although we take this pluralism for granted, it is instructive to remember how radical this concept was in the history of political philosophy. In the past, secular political philosophers argued that a legitimate state could not tolerate much freedom and diversity. After all, how would the dictator or monarch rule effectively if that much dissent were allowed?

Foundational to this idea is the belief that government should not be the final arbiter of truth. It should not be an institution that settles by force the truthfulness of an issue. This is why the framers of the Constitution specifically provided freedom of speech, freedom of the press, and freedom of religion. Government should not have power to impose its version of truth by force.

Christians should be strong supporters of this idea. We believe that God governs this world by His grace. His final judgment awaits, and we should not take His judgment into our hands. Overly anxious Christians often want to pull up the tares in the field instead of allowing the wheat and the tares to grow together.

Tyranny results when an authoritarian leader comes along who wants to impose his brand of truth on others. It is wrong for secularists to try to remove religion from the public sphere, and it is equally wrong for religious leaders to impose religion on others by force. In either case, the political arena becomes a religious battleground.

What we should develop is a civil debate where Christians are allowed to promote biblical morality without imposing it. This has been made more difficult by the current anti-religious climate in our society.

Richard John Neuhaus talks of the "naked public square," where religious values have been stripped from the public arenas of discourse. In this case, the tempered pluralism of the framers has been replaced by a radical pluralism that assumes that all values are relative. Public moral judgments, therefore, seem out of place. In recent years, we have seen a great deal of prejudice against such pronouncements simply because they are rooted in biblical morality.

Therefore, the "naked public square," where religious values are excluded, is wrong. Likewise, the "sacred public square," which seeks to impose religious values, is also wrong. What Christians should be arguing for is a "civil public square" that allows an open, civil debate to take place. In such an arena, controversial ideas can be discussed and debated in a civil manner.

This form of pluralism must be more than just window-dressing. Christians and non-Christians alike must be dedicated to maintaining a pluralism that allows vigorous interchange and debate. Unfortunately, there is some indication that many in our society see pluralism as merely a means to an end. English historian E. R. Norman believed that "pluralism is a name society gives itself when it is in the process of changing from one orthodoxy to another."

If this is what secularists really want, then pluralism is in trouble. When religion is excluded in the name of pluralism, then pluralism no longer exists.

Biblical Principles

Christians should first develop a comprehensive program of social involvement. The Lordship of Jesus Christ is not a temporary, issue-oriented crusade. Christians are not merely to march against injustice and then cease their involvement. They have an on-going responsibility to build positive alternatives to existing evil.

Second, social and political involvement based upon biblical absolutes must be realistic. We should not fall prey to utopian political philosophies but squarely face the sinful nature of man, and the important place government has in God's creation. Because of a general cynicism about the role of government, Christians are often guilty of neglecting their role in society.

As Christians, we must remember that although the times are evil, God's common grace restrains sin. Even though perfect justice cannot be achieved until Christ returns, we are nevertheless responsible for doing what we can. If we co-labor with God, we can have a measure of success in achieving a better society.

Third, Christians should focus attention not only on individual change but on societal change. Changing lives is fundamental but not completely sufficient to change society. Revival must lead to reformation. Christians should not merely be content with Christians thinking biblically about the issues of life. They must also be acting biblically and building institutions with a Christian framework. A Christian worldview implies a Christian world order.

Christian obedience goes beyond calling for spiritual renewal. We have often failed to ask the question: What do we do if hearts are not changed? Because government is ordained of God, we need to consider ways to use governmental power legitimately. Christians have a high stake in making sure government acts justly and makes decisions that provide maximum freedom for the furtherance of the gospel.

In situations in which governmental redress is not available, civil disobedience becomes an option. When such conditions exist, Christians might have to suffer the consequences as did their first-century counterparts in a hostile Roman culture.

We are to obey God rather than man (Acts 5:29) when civil government and civil law violate God's commands and law. Christians, therefore, were correct when they hid Jews from the Nazis during World War II. Hitler's Germany did not have the right to take innocent life or persecute the Jews.

Finally, the major focus of social involvement should be through the local church. Social action in the church is best called *social service* since it attempts to move from the theoretical area of social ethics to the practical level of serving others in need. While evangelicals are to be commended for giving to the poor and others faced with adversity, our duty does not stop there. A neglected area is a personal involvement with people who need help.

The local church is the best place to begin to meet many social needs of a society. In the New Testament, the local church was the training ground for social involvement and provided a context by which the needy were shown compassion. Christians, therefore, should begin their outreach to society from the church and work together to be the salt of the earth and the light of the world.

CHAPTER 10 Political Debate and Discernment

Turn on a television or open a newspaper. You are immediately presented with a myriad of ethical issues. Daily we are confronted with ethical choices and moral complexity. Society is awash in controversial issues: abortion, euthanasia, cloning, race, drug abuse, homosexuality, gambling, pornography, and capital punishment. Life may have been simpler in a previous age, but now the rise of technology and the fall of ethical consensus have brought us to a society full of moral dilemmas.

Biblical Ethics

Never has society needed biblical perspectives more to evaluate contemporary moral issues. And yet Christians seem less equipped to address these topics from a biblical perspective. The Barna Research Group conducted a national survey of adults and concluded that only four percent of adults have a biblical worldview as the basis of their decision-making. The survey also discovered that nine percent of born again Christians have such a perspective on life.[99]

It is worth noting that what George Barna defines as a biblical worldview would be considered by most people to be basic Christian doctrine. It doesn't even include aspects of a biblical perspective on social and political issues.

Of even greater concern is the fact that most Christians do not base their beliefs on an absolute moral

---

[99] "A Biblical Worldview Has a Radical Effect on a Person's Life," The Barna Update (Ventura, CA), 1 Dec. 2003.

foundation. Biblical ethics rests on the belief in absolute truth. Yet surveys show that a minority of born again adults (forty-four percent) and an even smaller proportion of born again teenagers (nine percent) are certain of the existence of absolute moral truth.[100] By a three-to-one margin adults say truth is always relative to the person and their situation. This perspective is even more lopsided among teenagers who overwhelmingly believe moral truth depends on the circumstances.[101]

Social scientists, as well as pollsters, have been warning that American society is becoming more and more dominated by moral anarchy. Writing in the early 1990s, James Patterson and Peter Kim said in *The Day America Told the Truth* that there was no moral authority in America. "We choose which laws of God we believe in. There is absolutely no moral consensus in this country as there was in the 1950s when all our institutions commanded more respect."[102] Essentially, we live in a world of moral anarchy.

So how do we begin to apply a Christian worldview to the complex social and political issues of the day? And how do we avoid falling for the latest fad or cultural trend that blows in the wind? The following are some key principles to apply and some dangerous pitfalls to avoid.

Biblical Principles

A key biblical principle that applies to the area of bioethics is the sanctity of human life. Such verses as

---

[100] "The Year's Most Intriguing Findings, From Barna Research Studies," The Barna Update (Ventura, CA), 12 Dec. 2000.

[101] "Americans Are Most Likely to Base Truth on Feelings," The Barna Update (Ventura, CA), 12 Feb. 2002.

[102] James Patterson and Peter Kim, *The Day America Told the Truth* (New York: Prentice Hall Press, 1991).

Psalm 139:13-16 show that God's care and concern extend to the womb. Other verses such as Jeremiah 1:5, Judges 13:7-8, Psalm 51:5 and Exodus 21:22–25 give additional perspective and framework to this principle. These principles can be applied to issues ranging from abortion to stem cell research to infanticide.

A related biblical principle involves the equality of human beings. The Bible teaches that God has made "of one blood all nations of men" (Acts 17:26). The Bible also teaches that it is wrong for a Christian to have feelings of superiority (Philippians 2). Believers are told not to make class distinctions between various people (James 2). Paul teaches the spiritual equality of all people in Christ (Galatians 3:28; Colossians 3:11). These principles apply to racial relations and our view of government.

A third principle is a biblical perspective on marriage. Marriage is God's plan and provides intimate companionship for life (Genesis 2:18). Marriage provides a context for the procreation and nurture of children (Ephesians 6:1-2). And finally, marriage provides a godly outlet for sexual desire (1 Corinthians 7:2). These principles can be applied to such diverse issues as artificial reproduction (which often introduces a third party into the pregnancy) and cohabitation (living together).

Another biblical principle involves sexual ethics. The Bible teaches that sex is to be within the bounds of marriage, as a man and the woman become one flesh (Ephesians 5:31). Paul teaches that we should "avoid sexual immorality" and learn to control our own body in a way that is "holy and honorable" (1 Thessalonians 4:3-5). He admonishes us to flee sexual immorality (1 Corinthians 6:18). These principles apply to such issues as premarital sex, adultery, and homosexuality.

A final principle concerns government and our obedience to civil authority. Government is ordained by

God (Rom.13:1-7). We are to render service and obedience to the government (Matt. 22:21) and submit to civil authority (1 Pet. 2:13-17). Even though we are to obey government, there may be certain times when we might be forced to obey God rather than men (Acts 5:29). These principles apply to issues such as war, civil disobedience, politics, and government.

Biblical Discernment

So how do we sort out what is true and what is false? This is a difficult proposition in a world awash in data. It underscores the need for Christians to develop discernment. This is a word that appears fairly often in the Bible (1 Samuel 25:32-33; 1 Kings 3:10-11; 4:29; Psalm 119:66; Proverbs 2:3; Daniel 2:14; Philippians 1:9 [NASB]). And with so many facts, claims, and opinions being tossed about, we all need to be able to sort through what is true and what is false.

Colossians 2:8 says, "See to it that no one takes you captive through philosophy and empty deception, according to the tradition of men, according to the elementary principles of the world, rather than according to Christ." We need to develop discernment so that we are not taken captive by false ideas. Here are some things to watch for:

1. Equivocation — the use of vague terms. Someone can start off using language we think we understand and then veer off into a new meaning. Most of us are well aware of the fact that religious cults are often guilty of this. A cult member might say that he believes in salvation by grace. But what he really means is that you have to join his cult and work your way toward salvation. Make people define the vague terms they use.

This tactic is frequently used in bioethics. Proponents of embryonic stem cell research often will not

95

acknowledge the distinction between adult stem cells and embryonic stem cells. Those trying to legalize cloning will refer to it as "somatic cell nuclear transfer." Unless you have a scientific background, you will not know that it is essentially the same thing.

2. Card stacking — the selective use of evidence. Don't jump on the latest bandwagon and intellectual fad without checking the evidence. Many advocates are guilty of listing all the points in their favor while ignoring the serious points against it.

The major biology textbooks used in high school and college never provide students with evidence against evolution. Jonathan Wells, in his book *Icons of Evolution*, shows that the examples that are used in most textbooks are either wrong or misleading.[103] Some of the examples are known frauds (such as the Haeckel embryos) and continue to show up in textbooks decades after they were shown to be fraudulent.

3. Appeal to authority — relying on authority to the exclusion of logic and evidence. Just because an expert says it, that doesn't necessarily make it true. We live in a culture that worships experts, but not all experts are right. Hiram's Law says: "If you consult enough experts, you can confirm any opinion."

Those who argue that global warming is caused by human activity often say that "the debate in the scientific community is over." But an Internet search of critics of the theories behind global warming will show that there are many scientists with credentials in climatology or meteorology who have questions about the theory. It is not accurate to say that the debate is over when the debate still seems to be taking place.

---

[103] Jonathan Wells, *Icons of Evolution: Science or Myth?* (Washington: Regnery Publishing, 2000).

4. Ad hominem — Latin for "against the man." People using this tactic attack the person instead of dealing with the validity of their argument. Often the soundness of an argument is inversely proportional to the amount of ad hominem rhetoric. If there is evidence for the position, proponents usually argue the merits of the position. When evidence is lacking, they attack the critics.

Christians who want public libraries to filter pornography from minors are accused of censorship. Citizens who want to define marriage as between one man and one woman are called bigots. Scientists who criticize evolution are subjected to withering attacks on their character and scientific credentials. Scientists who question global warming are compared to holocaust deniers.

5. Straw man argument — making your opponent's argument seem so ridiculous that it is easy to attack and knock down. Liberal commentators say that evangelical Christians want to implement a religious theocracy in America. That's not true. But the hyperbole works to marginalize Christian activists who believe they have a responsibility to speak to social and political issues within society.

Those who stand for moral principles in the area of bioethics often see this tactic used against them. They hear from proponents of physician-assisted suicide that pro-life advocates don't care about the suffering of the terminally ill. Proponents of embryonic stem cell research level the same charge by saying that pro-life people don't care that these new medical technologies could alleviate the suffering of many with intractable diseases. Nothing could be further from the truth.

6. Sidestepping — dodging the issue by changing the subject. Politicians do this in press conferences by not answering the question asked by the reporter, but instead answering a question they wish someone had asked.

Professors sometimes do that when a student points out an inconsistency or a leap in logic.

Ask a proponent of abortion whether the fetus is human and you are likely to see this tactic in action. He or she might start talking about a woman's right to choose or the right of women to control their own bodies. Perhaps you will hear a discourse on the need to tolerate various viewpoints in a pluralistic society. But you probably won't get a straight answer to an important question.

7. Red herring — going off on a tangent (from the practice of luring hunting dogs off the trail with the scent of a herring fish). Proponents of embryonic stem cell research rarely will talk about the morality of destroying human embryos. Instead, they will go off on a tangent and talk about the various diseases that could be treated and the thousands of people who could be helped with the research.

Be on the alert when someone in a debate changes the subject. They may want to argue their points on more familiar ground, or they may know they cannot win their argument on the relevant issue at hand.

In conclusion, we have discussed some of the key biblical principles we should apply to our consideration and debate about social and political issues. We have talked about the sanctity of human life and the equality of human beings. We have discussed a biblical perspective on marriage and on sexual ethics. And we have also talked about a biblical perspective on government and civil authority.

We have also spent some time talking about the importance of developing biblical discernment and looked at many of the logical fallacies that are frequently used in arguing against a biblical perspective on many of the social and political issues of our day.

Every day, it seems, we are confronted with ethical choices and moral complexity. As Christians, it is important to consider these biblical principles and consistently apply them to these issues. It is also important that we develop discernment and learn to recognize these tactics. We are called to develop discernment as we tear down false arguments raised up against the knowledge of God. By doing this, we will learn to take every thought captive to the obedience to Christ (2 Corinthians 10:4-5).

CHAPTER 11 Civil Disobedience

History of Civil Disobedience

Civil disobedience has a long history in the United States, starting with the American Revolution. Civil disobedience continued through the nineteenth century (the abolition movement protests preceding the Civil War) and surfaced in the latter part of the twentieth century in the civil rights movement, the environmental movement, and the peace movement (including protests against the Vietnam war and protests against nuclear arms). Today environmentalists, animal rights activists, or anti-government protesters sometimes use civil disobedience.

The modern debate on civil disobedience has been heavily influenced by the nineteenth-century writer Henry David Thoreau. Beginning from a humanistic perspective, he set forth a case for disobeying government. Thoreau wrote his famous essay "On the Duty of Civil Disobedience" after spending a night in the Concord, Massachusetts, jail in July 1846.[104] He had refused to pay his poll tax as a protest against a government that supported slavery. During the night someone paid the tax, and he was released. His essay grew out of his experience and has influenced many who consider similar actions. For example, Mahatma Gandhi printed and distributed Thoreau's essay and always carried a copy with him during his many imprisonments.

Thoreau challenged the prevailing notion of his day that obedience to government was more important than obedience to conscience. Most citizens would have argued that if a conflict existed between moral law and

---

[104] Henry David Thoreau, "On the Duty of Civil Disobedience" (n.p., 1849).

the government, one should obey government. Thoreau insisted that moral principle should come first and that civil disobedience was required even if it meant refusing to pay taxes or going to jail.

Thoreau's basic principle, however, leaves a question. Who is to decide when to disobey the government? According to Thoreau, each individual should follow his or her innate sense of goodness. Thus, each person must decide what he or she thinks is right and which laws he or she will obey or disobey. This moral anarchy resulted because he did not believe in an absolute standard of right and wrong.

Christians, however, have a transcendent set of standards to follow. The Bible lays out clear biblical principles that should be followed when a believer feels a conflict between God and government.

The best articulation of these biblical principles can be found in Samuel Rutherford's essay *Lex Rex*.[105] Arguing that governmental law was founded on the law of God, he rejected the seventeenth-century idea of the "divine right of kings." The king was not the ultimate authority; God's Law was (hence the title *Lex Rex*, "The law is king"). If the king and the government disobeyed the law, then they were to be disobeyed. Rutherford argued that all men, including the king, were under God's Law and not above it.

According to Rutherford, the civil magistrate was a "fiduciary figure" who held his authority in trust for the people. If that trust was violated, the people had a political basis for resistance. Not surprisingly *Lex Rex* was banned in England and Scotland and was seen as treasonous and fomenting political rebellion.

---

[105] Samuel Rutherford, Lex Rex or The Law and the Prince (n.p., 1644).

Biblical Examples of Civil Disobedience

In Romans 13:1-2 we read that; "Every person is to be in subjection to the governing authorities. For there is no authority except from God, and those which exist are established by God. Therefore whoever resists authority has opposed the ordinance of God; and they who have opposed will receive condemnation upon themselves." The Apostle Paul then concludes this section by saying that believers are to render to all what is due them: tax to whom tax is due; custom to whom custom; fear to whom fear; honor to whom honor.

The Apostle Peter likewise says, "Submit yourselves for the Lord's sake to every human institution, whether to a king as the one in authority, or to governors as sent by him for the punishment of evildoers and the praise of those who do right" (1 Pet. 2:13-14). Therefore, it is against this backdrop of biblical obedience to civil authorities that we discuss the issue of civil disobedience.

Francis Schaeffer said in the *Christian Manifesto* that if there is never a case in which a Christian would practice civil disobedience, then the state has become Lord. He said, "One either confesses that God is the final authority, or one confesses that Caesar is Lord. The Bible clearly teaches that there are times when a believer must disobey civil law so that he or she can obey God's higher law."[106]

The Bible provides a number of prominent examples of civil disobedience. When Pharaoh commanded the Hebrew midwives to kill all male Hebrew babies, they lied to Pharaoh and did not carry out his command (Exodus 1–2).

The Book of Daniel contains a number of instructive examples. For example, when Shadrach, Meshach, and

---

[106] Francis Schaeffer, *A Christian Manifesto* (Wheaton: Crossways, 1982), 91.

Abed-Nego refused to bow down to Nebuchadnezzar's golden image, they were cast into a fiery furnace (Daniel 3). The commissioners and satraps persuaded King Darius to decree that no one could petition any god or man for thirty days. Daniel nevertheless continued to pray to God three times a day and was cast into the lion's den (Daniel 6).

The most dramatic example of civil disobedience in the New Testament is recorded in Acts 4–5. When Peter and John were commanded not to preach the gospel, their response was, "We must obey God rather than men" (5:29).

These examples each included at least two common elements. First, a direct, specific conflict arose between God's law and man's law. Pharaoh commanded the Hebrew midwives to kill male Hebrew babies. Nebuchadnezzar commanded his subjects to bow before the golden image. King Darius ruled that no one could pray. And in the New Testament the high priest and the Sanhedrin forbade the apostles from proclaiming the gospel.

Second, in choosing to obey God's higher law, believers paid the normal consequence for disobedience. Although several of them escaped the consequence through supernatural intervention, we know from biblical and secular history of many others who paid for their disobedience with their lives.

Some critics argue that Romans 13:1 clearly prohibits civil disobedience: "Everyone must submit himself to the governing authorities, for there is no authority except that which God has established." Yet even this passage seems to provide a possible argument for disobeying government that has exceeded its authority. The verses following these speak of the government's role and function. The ruler is to be a "servant of God" and government should reward good and punish evil.

Government that fails to do so is outside of God's mandated authority and function.

The apostle Paul called for believers to "be subject" to government, but he did not instruct them to "obey" every command of government. When government commands an unjust or unbiblical injunction, Christians have a higher authority. One can be "subject" to the authority of the state but still refuse to "obey" a specific law that is contrary to biblical standards.

Biblical Principles for Civil Disobedience

How should Christians engage in civil disobedience? Here are five principles that should guide an individual's decision about civil disobedience.

First, the law or injunction being resisted should clearly be unjust and unbiblical. Christians are not allowed to resist laws merely because they disagree with them. Given our sin nature and our natural tendency toward anarchy, it seems appropriate for Christians to make a strong case for civil disobedience before they act. The burden of proof should be on the person advocating civil disobedience. In a sense, we should be talked into disobedience. If the case is not compelling for civil disobedience, then obedience is required by default.

Second, the means of redress should be exhausted. One of the criteria for a just war is that the recourse to war must be the last resort. Civil disobedience should follow the same rigorous criterion. When all recourse to civil obedience has been exhausted, then and only then can discussion of revolution begin. Even then minimum resistance should be used if it can achieve a just result. If peaceful means can be used, then force should be avoided. Only when all legal channels for change have been closed or exhausted should civil disobedience be seriously considered. The only exception may be when the injustice is so grave and immediate that time for lengthy appeals is impossible.

Third, Christians must be willing to accept the penalty for breaking the law. The various biblical examples mentioned provide a model for Christian behavior in the midst of civil disobedience. Christians should submit to authority even when disobeying government. Such an attitude distinguishes civil disobedience from anarchy. By accepting the punishment, believers can often provide a powerful testimony to non-believers and awaken their concern for the injustice.

Fourth, civil disobedience should be carried out in love and with humility. Disobeying government should not be done with an angry or rebellious spirit. Martin Luther King, Jr., taught that "whom you would change you must first love."[107] Bringing about social change requires love, patience, and humility, not anger and arrogance.

A fifth and more controversial principle is that civil disobedience should be considered only when there is some possibility for success. Another criteria for a just war is that there be some reasonable hope of success. In the case of civil disobedience success is not an ultimate criterion, but it should be a concern if true social change is to take place. An individual certainly is free to disobey a law for personal reasons, but any attempt to change a law or social situation should enlist the aid and support of others.

Christians should prayerfully evaluate whether the social disruption and potential promotion of lawlessness that may ensue is worth the action of civil disobedience. In most cases, Christians will be more effective by working within the social and political arenas to affect true social change.

---

[107] Martin Luther King, Jr. quoted in Richard John Neuhaus, *Naked Public Square* (Grand Rapids: Eerdmans, 1984), 237.

SECTION 5 Christian Heritage

CHAPTER 12 On Two Wings

Michael Novak has been and continues to be one of the most influential intellectuals of our time. The author of more than thirty books, he has been a professor at Harvard, Stanford, and Notre Dame and was awarded the $1 million Templeton Prize for Progress in Religion.

So it is significant that his book, On Two Wings, documents the Judeo-Christian foundations of this country and disputes the teaching that the American Founders were secular Enlightenment rationalists. Instead, he persuasively argues that they were the creators of a unique American blend of biblical faith, practical reason, and human liberty.

In his preface, Michael Novak says, "Although I have wanted to write this book for some forty years, my own ignorance stood in the way. It took me a long time, time spent searching up many byways and neglected paths, and fighting through a great deal of conventional (but mistaken) wisdom, to learn how many erroneous perceptions I had unconsciously drunk in from public discussion."[108]

Novak believes that "most of us grow up these days remarkably ignorant of the hundred men most responsible for leading this country into a War for Independence and writing our nation's Constitution."[109]

The way American history has been told for the last century is incomplete. Secular historians have "cut off one of the two wings by which the American eagle flies." The founding generation established a compact with the God

---

[108] Michael Novak, On Two Wings: Humble Faith and Common Sense at the American Founding (San Francisco: Encounter, 2002), 1

[109] Ibid.

of Israel "and relied upon this belief. Their faith is an *indispensable* part of their story."[110]

Historical research by a number of scholars documents the significant influence of the Bible on the founders. Two decades ago, Constitutional scholars and political historians (including one of my professors at Georgetown University) assembled 15,000 writings from the Founding Era. They counted 3154 citations in these writings. They found that the two political philosophers most often quoted were Montesquieu and Blackstone. But surprisingly, the reference most quoted was the Bible. It was quoted 34 percent of the time. This was nearly four times as often as Montesquieu or Blackstone and 12 times more often than John Locke was.

While secular historians point to Locke as the source of the ideas embodied in Thomas Jefferson's Declaration of Independence, they usually fail to note the older influence of other authors and the Bible. "Before Locke was even born, the Pilgrims believed in the consent of the governed, social compacts, the dignity of every child of God, and political equality."[111] By forcing a secular interpretation onto America's founding history, these secular historians ignore the second wing by which the American eagle took flight.

Philosophical Assumptions of the Founders of this Country

First, the Bible was the one book that literate Americans in the 18th century could be expected to know well. Biblical imagery was a central part of American life. For example, Thomas Jefferson suggested as a design for the Seal of the United States a representation of the

---

[110] Ibid., 5.

[111] Ibid., 6-7.

108

children of Israel in the wilderness, led by a cloud by day and pillar of fire by night.

Second, the founders believed that time "was created for the *unfolding of human liberty*, for human emancipation. This purpose requires humans to choose for or against building cities worthy of the ideals God sets before them: liberty, justice, equality, self-government, and brotherhood."[112]

The first paragraph of *The Federalist* describes this important moment with destiny:

> It seems to have been reserved to the people of this country, by their conduct and example, to decide the important question, whether societies of men are really capable or not of establishing good government from reflection and choice, or whether they are forever destined to depend for their political constitutions on accident and force.[113]

The founders believed that they could learn from history and put together piece by piece what they called "an improved science of politics." History, they believed, was a record of progress (or decline) measured against God's standards and learned from personal and historical experience.

Third, the founders also held that everything in creation was intelligible and thus discernible through reason and rational evaluation. They also believed that God was The Creator and thus gave us life and liberty. Thomas Jefferson said, "The God Who gave us life gave us liberty at the same time."

---

[112] Ibid., 8-9.

[113] *The Federalist Papers*, Number 1.

Novak concludes that without this philosophical foundation, "the founding generation of Americans would have had little heart for the War of Independence. They would have had no ground for believing that their seemingly unlawful rebellion actually fulfilled the will of God — and suited the laws of nature and nature's God. Consider the jeopardy in which their rebellion placed them: When they signed the Declaration, they were committing treason in the King's eyes. If their frail efforts failed, their flagrant betrayal of the solemn oaths of loyalty they had sworn to their King doomed them to a public hanging. Before future generations, their children would be disgraced. To still their trembling, they pled their case before a greater and wholly undeceivable Judge, appealing to the Supreme Judge of the world for the Rectitude of our Intentions."[114]

Seven Events in the Founding of this Country

The first event was the first act of the First Continental Congress in September 1774. When the delegates gathered in Philadelphia, their purpose was to remind King George of the rights due them as Englishmen. But as they gathered, news arrived that Charlestown had been raked by cannon shot while red-coated landing parties surged through its streets.

The first motion of the Congress proposed a public prayer. Some of the delegates spoke against the motion because, they argued, Americans were so divided in religious sentiments (Episcopalians, Quakers, Anabaptists, Presbyterians, Congregationalists). Sam Adams arose to say he was no bigot and could hear the prayer from any gentleman of piety and virtue. He proposed that Reverend Duch had earned that character.

---

[114] Novak, *Wings*, 12.

The next day, a white-haired Episcopal clergyman dressed in his pontificals pronounced the first official prayer before the Continental Congress. Before this priest knelt men like Washington, Henry, Randolph, Rutledge, Lee, and Jay. The emotion in the room was palpable. John Adams wrote to his wife Abigail that he "had never heard a better prayer, or one so well pronounced." He went on to say that, it was "enough to melt a heart of stone. I saw tears gush into the eyes of the old, grave pacific Quakers of Philadelphia."[115]

The second event was the sermon by John Witherspoon of Princeton on May 17, 1776. In this pivotal sermon, Witherspoon who had opposed the rebellion went over to the side of independence. His influence cannot be overstated. He was James Madison's teacher, and he is credited with having taught one vice-president, twelve members of the Continental Congress, five delegates to the Constitutional Convention, forty-nine U.S. representatives, twenty-eight U.S. Senators, three Supreme Court justices, and scores of officers in the Continental Army. His sermons were printed in over 500 Presbyterian churches throughout the colonies.

His message centered on the doctrine of divine providence. He argued that even things that seem harmful and destructive may be turned to the advantage of the patriots. Even the enemies of law and morality cannot escape being the instruments of Providence. Witherspoon argued that liberty is God's gift, and all of creation has been contrived so that out of darkness and despair, freedom will come to fruition.

Michael Novak concludes that "During the years 1770-1776, the fires of revolution were lit by Protestant divines aflame with the dignity of human conscience. 'To

---

[115] William Federer, ed. *America's God and Country* (Coppell: TX: FAME, 1994), 137.

the Pulpit, the Puritan Pulpit,' wrote John Wingate Thornton, 'We owe the moral force which won our independence.'"[116]

The third event was the writing of the Declaration of Independence. Its very form was that of a traditional American prayer, similar to the Mayflower Compact. In essence, it was only the latest in a long series of local and regional covenants which put all governmental bodies on notice by establishing a national compact.

The fifty-six signers of the Declaration were mostly Christian and represented mostly Christian people. The four names that these signers gave to God were: Lawgiver (as in "Laws of Nature and Nature's God"), Creator ("endowed by their Creator with certain inalienable rights"), Judge ("appealing to the Supreme Judge of the World for the Rectitude of our Intentions"), and Providence ("with a firm Reliance on the Protection of divine Providence").

Novak points out that: "Three of these names (Creator, Judge, Providence) unambiguously derive from Judaism and came to America via Protestant Christianity. The fourth name for God, 'Lawgiver,' could be considered Greek or Roman as well as Hebraic. But Richard Hooker showed that long tradition had put 'Lawgiver,' too, in a Biblical context."[117]

The fourth event was a national day of prayer. Only five months after the Declaration, "the pinch and suffering of war and a poor harvest seriously imperiled morale." Congress set aside December 11, 1776, as a Day of Fasting and Repentance.

The fifth event occurred when George Washington became commander of the amateurs who became the

---

[116] Novak, *Wings*, 17.

[117] Ibid., 17-18.

Continental Army. He knew he had to prepare them for the adversity to come. "To stand with swollen chests in a straight line, beneath snapping flags, to the music of fife and drums is one thing; to hold your place when the British musketballs roar toward you like a wall of blazing lead, and all around you the flesh of screaming friends and brothers is shredded, is another."[118]

Washington knew there would be bitter winters and hot summers with no pay and little food. Often the soldiers would have to frequently retreat rather than face frontal combat from the enemy. He knew his only hope was to fashion a godly corps whose faith was placed in the Creator not battlefield victories. So Washington gave orders that each day begin with formal prayer, to be led by officers of each unit. He also ordered that officers of every unit "to procure Chaplains according to the decree of the Continental Congress." Washington knew that prayer and spiritual discipline were essential to his army's success.

The sixth event occurred toward the end of the fighting season in late August, 1776. George Washington had assembled 12,000 local militiamen of the Continental Army on Long Island. British Generals Howe, Clinton, Cornwallis, and Percy along with the German Major General von Heister landed a royal detachment twice as large to the rear of the Continental Army. The British took up positions to march swiftly toward the East River to trap Washington's entire army and put an end to the American insurrection.

Seeing that they might lose everything, Washington put out a call for every available vessel so that he might ferry his troops by cover of night back to Manhattan. All night the men scoured for boats, marched in silence, and rowed. But by dawn, only a fraction had made their

---

[118] Ibid., 19.

escape. The Americans prepared for the worst. As if in answer to their prayers, a heavy fog rolled in and lasted until noon.

By the time the fog lifted, the entire Army escaped. Many gave thanks to God. And Washington and many others considered it one of those "signal interventions" by Divine Providence that saved the army and allowed the revolution to continue.

The seventh event was the establishment of Thanksgiving near the end of the third year of the war. Congress had many reasons to express thanksgiving to God and to seek His continued mercy and assistance. John Witherspoon was called upon to draft a Thanksgiving Day recollection of those events. The Congress urged the nation to "humbly approach the throne of Almighty God" to ask "that he would establish the independence of these United States upon the basis of religion and virtue."

Following the wartime precedent of the Congress, Washington issued his first Thanksgiving Day Proclamation shortly after becoming president in 1789. He reminded the nation of God's protection and provision in the Battle of Long Island all the way to their victory at Yorktown. Years later Abraham Lincoln, after annual presidential proclamations of Thanksgiving waned, reinstituted a national day of Thanksgiving on November 26, 1863 and the tradition has continued ever since.

Michael Novak has provided Americans with a great service in documenting the Christian influence in the founding of this country. This religious influence is the second wing that tapped into the deepest energies of the human spirit and propelled this nation forward through difficult times and great challenges.

It is also fitting that we remember these important religious concepts and their influence on our nation. If we take seriously the words of George Washington in his Farewell Address to the Nation, then our ignorance of our nation's past may yet be our destruction. That is why we must study our history and teach it correctly to the next generation so we may keep the torch of freedom alive for generations to come.

CHAPTER 13 One Nation Under God

Founders of America

G.K. Chesterton once said that: "America is the only nation in the world that is founded on a creed. That creed is set forth with dogmatic and even theological lucidity in the Declaration of Independence."[119] We are going to document the origins of this country by looking at a book entitled *One Nation Under God: Ten Things Every Christian Should Know About the Founding of America.*[120]

The first thing every Christian should know is that "Christopher Columbus was motivated by his Christian faith to sail to the New World." One example of this can be found in his writings after he discovered this new land. He wrote, "Therefore let the king and queen, the princes and their most fortunate kingdoms, and all other countries of Christendom give thanks to our Lord and Saviour Jesus Christ, who has bestowed upon us so great a victory and gift. Let religious processions be solemnized; let sacred festivals be given; let the churches be covered with festive garlands. Let Christ rejoice on earth, as he rejoices in heaven when he foresees coming to salvation so many souls of people hitherto lost."[121]

The second thing every Christian should know is "The Pilgrims clearly stated that they came to the New World to glorify God and to advance the Christian faith."

---

[119] Gilbert K. Chesterton, *What I Saw in America* (London: Hodder and Stoughton, 1922).

[120] David C. Gibbs and Jerry Newcombe, *One Nation Under God: Ten Things Every Christian Should Know About the Founding of America* (Seminole, FL: Christian Law Association, 2003).

[121] Christopher Columbus, Journal, 1492, quoted in Federer, United States Folder, *Library of Classics.*

It could easily be said that America began with the words, "In the name of God. Amen." Those were the first words of our nation's first self-governing document—the Mayflower Compact.

The Pilgrims were Bible-believers who refused to conform to the heretical state Church of England and eventually came to America. Their leader, William Bradford, said "A great hope and inward zeal they had of laying some good foundation, or at least to make some way thereunto, for the propagating and advancing the gospel of the kingdom of Christ in those remote parts of the world; yea, though they should be but even as stepping stones unto others for the performing of so great a work."[122]

Many scholars believe that the initial agreement for self- government, found in the Mayflower Compact, became the cornerstone of the U.S. Constitution. This agreement for self-government, signed on November 11, 1620, created a new government in which they agreed to "covenant and combine" themselves together into a "Body Politick."

British historian Paul Johnson said, "It is an amazing document . . . . What was remarkable about this particular contract was that it was not between a servant and a master, or a people and a king, but between a group of like-minded individuals and each other, with God as a witness and symbolic co-signatory."[123]

The third thing every Christian should know is "The Puritans created Bible-based commonwealths in order to practice a representative government that was modeled on their church covenants." Both the Pilgrims and the

---

[122] William Bradford, *Of Plymouth Plantation*, 1620-1647, edited and updated by Samuel Eliot Morison (New York: Alfred A. Knopf, 2001), 25.

[123] Paul Johnson, *A History of the American People* (New York: HarperCollins Publishers, 1997), 29-30.

Puritans disagreed with many things about the Church of England in their day. But the Pilgrims felt that reforming the church was a hopeless endeavor. They were led to separate themselves from the official church and were often labeled "Separatists." The Puritans, on the other hand, wanted to reform the Church of England from within. They argued from within for purity of the church, and therefore were called *the Puritans*.

At that time, there had been no written constitution in England. The British common law was a mostly oral tradition, articulated as necessary in various written court decisions. The Puritans determined to anchor their liberties on the written page, a tradition taken from the Bible. They created the Body of Liberties, which were established on the belief, that Christ's rule is not only given for the church, but also for the state. It contained principles found in the Bible, specifically ninety-eight separate protections of individual rights, including due process of law, trial by a jury of peers, and prohibitions against cruel and unusual punishment.

The fourth thing every Christian should know is that "This nation was founded as a sanctuary for religious dissidents." Roger Williams questioned many of the Puritan laws in Massachusetts, especially the right of magistrates to punish Sabbath-breakers. After he left Massachusetts and founded Rhode Island, he became the first to formulate the concept of "separation of church and state" in America.

Williams said, "The civil magistrate may not intermeddle even to stop a church from apostasy and heresy."[124] In the 1643 charter for Rhode Island and in all its subsequent charters, Roger Williams established the idea that the state should not enforce religious opinion.

---

[124] George Bancroft, *History of the United States of America, From the Discovery of the Continent* (New York: D. Appleton and Company, 1890), Vol. I, 250.

Another dissident was the Quaker William Penn. He was the main author of the founding governmental document for the land that came to be known as Pennsylvania. This document was called *The Concessions*, and dealt with not only government matters but was also concerned with social, philosophical, scientific, and political matters. By 1680, *The Concessions* had 150 signers, and in the Quaker spirit, this group effort provided for far-reaching liberties never before seen in Anglo-Saxon law.

Paul Johnson said that at the time of America's founding, Philadelphia was "the cultural capital of America." He also points out: "It can be argued, indeed, that Quaker Pennsylvania was the key state in American history. It was the last great flowering of Puritan political innovation, around its great city of brotherly love."[125]

Education and Religion in America

The fifth thing every Christian should know is that "The education of the settlers and founders of America was uniquely Christian and Bible-based." Education was very important to the founders of this country. One of the laws in Puritan New England was the Old Deluder Act. It was called that because it was intended to defeat Satan, the Old Deluder, who had used illiteracy in the Old World to keep people from reading the Word of God. The New England Primer was used to teach colonial children to read and included the Lord's Prayer, the Apostle's Creed, and the text of many hymns and prayers.

We can also see the importance of education in the rules of many of the first colleges. The Laws and Statutes of Harvard College in 1643 said: "Let every student be plainly instructed and earnestly pressed to consider well

---

[125] Johnson, 66.

119

the main end of his life and studies is *to know God and Jesus Christ which is eternal life* (John 17:3)."[126]

Yale College listed two requirements in its 1745 charter: "All scholars shall live religious, godly, and blameless lives according to the rules of God's Word, diligently reading the Holy Scriptures, the fountain of light and truth; and constantly attend upon all the duties of religion, both in public and secret."[127]

Reverend John Witherspoon was the only active minister who signed the Declaration of Independence. Constitutional scholar John Eidsmoe says, "John Witherspoon is best described as the man who shaped the men who shaped America. Although he did not attend the Constitutional Convention, his influence was multiplied many times over by those who spoke as well as by what was said."[128]

New Jersey elected John Witherspoon to the Continental Congress that drafted the Declaration of Independence. When Congress called for a national day of fasting and prayer on May 17, 1776, John Witherspoon was called upon to preach the sermon. His topic was "The Dominion of Providence over the Affairs of Men."

The sixth thing every Christian should know is that "A religious revival was the key factor in uniting the separate pre- Revolutionary War colonies."

Paul Johnson, author of *A History of the American People*, reports that the Great Awakening may have touched as many as three out of four American

---

[126] Rules for Harvard University, 1643, from "New England's First Fruits," *The Annals of America*, Vol. 1, 176.

[127] Regulations at Yale College, 1745, from "New England's First Fruits," *The Annals of America*, Vol. 1, 464.

[128] John Eidsmoe, *Christianity and the Constitution* (Grand Rapids, MI: Baker Books, 1987), 81.

colonists.[129] He also points out that this Great Awakening "sounded the death-knell of British colonialism."[130]

As John Adams was to put it afterward, "The Revolution was effected before the War commenced. The Revolution was in the mind and hearts of the people: and change in their religious sentiments of their duties and obligations."

Paul Johnson believes that "The Revolution could not have taken place without this religious background. The essential difference between the American Revolution and the French Revolution is that the American Revolution, in its origins, was a religious event, whereas the French Revolution was an anti-religious event."[131]

Clergy and Biblical Christianity

The seventh thing every Christian should know is that "Many of the clergy in the American colonies, members of the Black Regiment, preached liberty." Much of this took place in so-called "Election Sermons" of Massachusetts, Connecticut, New Hampshire, and Vermont. Often the ministers spoke on the subject of civil government in a serious and instructive manner. The sermon was then printed so that every representative had a copy for himself, and so that every minister of the town could have a copy.

John Adams observed, "The Philadelphia ministers thunder and lighten every Sabbath' against George III's despotism."[132] And in speaking of his native Virginia,

---

[129] Johnson, 115.

[130] Ibid., 307.

[131] Ibid., 116-117.

[132] Derek Davis, "Jesus vs. the Watchmaker," *Christian History*, May 1996, 35.

Thomas Jefferson observed that: "pulpit oratory ran like a shock of electricity through the whole colony."[133]

Some of the most influential preachers include John Witherspoon, Jonathan Mayhew, Samuel West, and Reverend John Peter Muhlenberg. Reverend Mayhew, for example, preached a message entitled "Concerning Unlimited Submission to the Higher Powers, to the Council and House of Representatives in Colonial New England." He said, "It is hoped that but few will think the subject of it an improper one to be discoursed on in the pulpit, under a notion that this is preaching politics, instead of Christ. However, to remove all prejudices of this sort, I beg it may be remembered that all Scripture is profitable for doctrine, for reproof, for correction, for instruction in righteousness.' Why, then, should not those parts of Scripture which related to civil government be examined and explained from the desk, as well as others?"[134]

The eighth thing every Christian should know is that "Biblical Christianity was the driving force behind the key leaders of the American Revolution."

In 1772, Samuel Adams created a "Committee of Correspondence" in Boston, in order to keep in touch with his fellow Americans up and down the coast. Historian George Bancroft called Sam Adams, "the last of the Puritans."[135] His biographer, John C. Miller, says that Samuel Adams cannot be understood without considering the lasting impact Whitefield's preaching at Harvard during the Great Awakening had on him.[136] Adams had

---

[133] Thomas Jefferson, *Autobiography*, January 6, 1821.

[134] Jonathan Mayhew, to the Council and House of Representatives in Colonial New England, 1749.

[135] Bancroft, History, Vol. III, 77.

[136] John C. Miller, *Sam Adams: Pioneer in Propaganda* (Stanford, CA: Stanford University Press, 1936/1960), 85, quoted in Eidsmoe, *Christianity and the Constitution*, 248.

been telling his countrymen for years that America had to take her stand against tyranny. He regarded individual freedom as "the law of the Creator" and a Christian right documented in the New Testament.[137] As the Declaration was being signed, Sam Adams said, "We have this day restored the Sovereign to Whom all men ought to be obedient. He reigns in heaven and from the rising to the setting of the sun, let His kingdom come."

The Founding Documents

The ninth thing every Christian should know is that "Christianity played a significant role in the development of our nation's birth certificate, the Declaration of Independence." For example, the Presbyterian Elders of North Carolina drafted the Mecklenburg Declaration in May 1775 under the direction of Elder Ephraim Brevard (a graduate of Princeton). One scholar says "In correcting his first draft of the Declaration it can be seen, in at least a few places, that Jefferson has erased the original words and inserted those which are first found in the Mecklenburg Declaration. No one can doubt that Jefferson had Brevard's resolutions before him when he was writing his immortal Declaration."[138]

The relationship between the Declaration of Independence and the Constitution is crucial. The Declaration is the "why" of American government, while the Constitution is the "how."

Another influence on the Declaration was George Mason's "Virginia Declaration of Rights." Notice how similar it sounds to the Declaration: "That all men are by nature equally free and independent and have certain

---

[137] Robert Flood, *Men Who Shaped America* (Chicago: Moody Press, 1976), 35-36.

[138] N. S. McFetridge, *Calvinism in History* (Philadelphia: Presbyterian Board of Publication, 1882), 85-88.

inherent rights, of which, when they enter into a state of society, they cannot, by any compact, deprive or divest their posterity; namely, the enjoyment of life and liberty, with the means of acquiring and possessing property, and pursuing and obtaining happiness and safety."

Paul Johnson says, "There is no question that the Declaration of Independence was, to those who signed it, a religious as well as secular act, and that the Revolutionary War had the approbation of divine providence. They had won it with God's blessing and afterwards, they drew up their framework of government with God's blessing, just as in the seventeenth century the colonists had drawn up their Compacts and Charters and Orders and Instruments, with God peering over their shoulders."[139]

The tenth thing every Christian should know is that "The Biblical understanding of the sinfulness of man was the guiding principle behind the United States Constitution." John Eidsmoe says, "Although Witherspoon derived the concept of separation of powers from other sources, such as Montesquieu, checks and balances seem to have been his own unique contribution to the foundation of U.S. Government."[140] He adds, "One thing is certain: the Christian religion, particularly Rev. Witherspoon's Calvinism, which emphasized the fallen nature of man, influenced Madison's view of law and government."[141]

Christian principles were important in the founding of this country and important in framing our government. If they were so important in the founding of this republic, certainly they should also be important in the maintenance of this republic.

---

[139] Johnson, 204-205.

[140] Eidsmoe, 89.

[141] Ibid., 101.

Bibliography

Amos, Gary. *Defending the Declaration*. Brentwood, TN: Wolgemuth and Hyatt, 1989.

Bancroft, George. *History of the United States of America, From the Discovery of the Continent*. New York:: D. Appleton and Company, 1890.

Bradford, M. E. *A Worthy Company: Brief Lives of the Framers of the United States Constitution*. Marlborough, NH: Plymouth Rock Foundation, 1982.

Bradford, William. *Of Plymouth Plantation, 1620-1647, edited and updated by Samuel Eliot Morison*. New York: Alfred A. Knopf, 2001.

Chesterton, Gilbert K. *What I Saw in America*. London: Hodder and Stoughton, 1922.

Cooke, Jacob E. *The Federalist*. Middletown, CT: Wesleyan University Press, 1961.

Danford, John W. *Roots of Freedom: A Primer on Modern Liberty*. Wilmington, DE: ISI Books, 2000.

Dreisbach, Daniel. *Thomas Jefferson and the Wall of Separation Between Church and State*. New York: New York University Press, 2002.

Dwight, Timothy. *The Duty of Americans, at the Present Crisis, reprinted in Ellis Sandoz, ed., Political Sermons of the American Founding Era, 1730-1805*. Indianapolis, IN: Liberty Press, 1991.

Eidsmoe, John. *Christianity and the Constitution*. Grand Rapids, MI: Baker Books, 1987.

Federer, William ed. *America's God and Country*. Coppell: TX: FAME, 1994.

Flood, Robert. *Men Who Shaped America*. Chicago: Moody Press, 1976.

Gaustad, Edwin. *Sworn on the Altar of God: A Religious Biography of Thomas Jefferson*. Grand Rapids, Mich: William B Eerdmans, 1996.

Gibbs, David C, and Jerry Newcombe. *One Nation Under God: Ten Things Every Christian Should Know About the Founding of America*. Seminole, FL: Christian Law Association, 2003.

Hamburger, Philip. *Separation of Church and State*. Cambridge, MA: Harvard University Press, 2002.

Hamilton, Alexander. *The Federalist Papers*. New York: New American Library, 1961.

Hobbes, Thomas. *Leviathan*. Indianapolis: Hackett Publishing, 1994.

House, Wayne ed.,. *Restoring The Constitution*. Dallas, TX: Probe Books, 1987.

Hutchins, Robert M. *"The Future of the Wall," in The Wall between Church and State, ed. Dallin H. Oaks*. Chicago: University of Chicago Press, 1963.

Jay, John. *October 12, 1816, in The Correspondence and Public Papers of John Jay, Henry P. Johnston, ed., Vol. IV*. New York: G.P Putnam & Sons, 1893, reprinted NY: Burt Franklin 1970.

Johnson, Paul. *A History of the American People*. New York: HarperCollins Publishers, 1997.

Locke, John. *Two Treatises of Government, ed. Peter Laslett*. Cambridge: Cambridge University Press, 1960.

Lutz, Donald S. *The Origins of American Constitutionalism*. Baton Rouge: Louisiana State University Press, 1988.

126

Madison, James. *Federalist, #51.* New York: New American Library, 1961.

Malone, Dumas. *Jefferson and His Time, vol. 3, Jefferson and the Ordeal of Liberty.* Boston: Little, Brown, 1962.

McFetridge, N. S. *Calvinism in History.* Philadelphia: Presbyterian Board of Publication, 1882.

Miller, John C, and Sam Adams. *Pioneer in Propaganda (, CA: , .* Stanford, CA: Stanford University Press, 1936/1960.

Monsma, Stephen V. *Positive Neutrality.* Grand Rapids, MI: Baker Books, 1993.

Neuhaus, Richard John. *Martin Luther King, Jr. quoted in Richard John Neuhaus, Naked Public Square.* Grand Rapids: Eerdmans, 1984.

—. *The Naked Public Square: Religion and Democracy in America.* Grand Rapids: William B. Eerdmans Publishing Co., 1984.

Novak, Michael. *On Two Wings: Humble Faith and Common Sense at the American Founding.* San Francisco: Encounter, 2002.

Patterson, James, and Peter Kim. *The Day America Told the Truth.* New York: Prentice Hall Press, 1991.

Penn, William. *April 25, 1682, in the preface of his Frame of Government of Pennsylvania. A Collection of Charters and Other Public Acts Relating to the Province of Pennsylvania.* Philadelphia: B. Franklin, 1740.

Perry, Barbara. ""Justice Hugo Black and the Wall of Separation between Church and State"." *Journal of Church and State 31,* 1989: 55.

Rossiter, Clinton. *The Federalist Papers*. New York: New American Library, 1961.

Rush, Benjamin. *"Thoughts upon the Mode of Education Proper in a Republic," Early American Imprints. Benjamin Rush, Essays, Literary, Moral and Philosophical* . Philadelphia: Thomas and Samuel F. Bradford, 1798.

Schaeffer, Francis. *A Christian Manifesto*. Wheaton: Crossways, 1982.

Singer, C. Gregg. *A Theological Interpretation of American History*. Nutley, NJ: The Craig Press, 1964.

Storing, Herbert, and Murray, eds. Day. *The Complete Anti-Federalist*. Chicago: University of Chicago Press, 1981.

Webster, Daniel. *December 22, 1820. The Works of Daniel Webster*. Boston: Little, Brown and Company, 1853.

Wells, Jonathan. *Icons of Evolution: Science or Myth?* Washington: Regnery Publishing, 2000.

Whitehead, John. *The Separation Illusion*. Milford, MI: Mott Media, 1977.

Williams, Roger. *"Mr. Cotton's Letter Lately Printed, Examined and Answered," in The Complete Writings of Roger Williams*. Providence, RI: Providence Press, 1866.